A POWERFUL TEAM

How CEOs and
Their HR Leaders
Are Transforming
Organizations

SCOTT ROSEN, DAVID PINETTE, AND JOHN TOUEY

authorHOUSE®

AuthorHouse™
1663 Liberty Drive
Bloomington, IN 47403
www.authorhouse.com
Phone: 1 (800) 839-8640

Published by AuthorHouse 03/07/2017

ISBN: 978-1-5246-7451-9 (sc)
ISBN: 978-1-5246-7450-2 (e)

Library of Congress Control Number: 2017903243

Print information available on the last page.

Table of Contents

Acknowledgment

We would like to thank Al Desetta, whose writing and editing skills were instrumental in the completion of this book. Visit his websites: www.aldesetta.com and www.ghostwritingbooks4u.com.

Introduction

Why HR Matters More than Ever

A Powerful Team shows why HR strategy matters and how it can mean the difference between organizational success and failure. Based on interviews with top CEOs and HR leaders, this book makes the compelling argument that an effective HR strategy can lead to transformative improvements in your business approach and bottom line. The advice contained herein—a collection of "best practices" on how to make the most of HR—is based on the hard-earned experience of business leaders from large, medium, and smaller companies in various industries, both public and private.

CEOs tend to fall into two categories. One group believes HR plays a defensive role focused on compliance, regulation, and administration. The other group believes that HR can really help drive organizational transformation and performance.

Many of the CEOs and CHROs we interviewed were once skeptical about HR's strategic power. Others were wary of the softer side of HR, its role in establishing mission, vision, and values. But all are now true believers that HR, properly harnessed, has been a central factor in driving dramatic and permanent change within their companies. What was once a relative backwater that handled benefits, compensation, and employee relations is now, in their view, a force equal in power to any of their business units.

"When you're new in business, you view HR through three lenses— hiring, benefits, and payroll," said one of the CEOs we interviewed. "Early in my career, that was how I saw HR—you went to them when you wanted to change a dependent or when your paycheck wasn't right. [But] as you start to mature as a leader…your view of HR becomes much more strategic."

"Like most people," another CEO told us, "I didn't see the point of talking to HR about how to grow the business. We talked to HR only when someone had a performance problem or was in trouble in some way. My view changed when I took on a leadership position in operations and headquarters."

Perhaps you've been one of the skeptics. Perhaps, as the CEO or senior member of the executive team, you've had these thoughts:

"I'm not sure I see the value in my HR leader or function. HR doesn't get the connection to business results. They're a little too divorced from what actually drives the company."

"I'm not sure what ROI I'm getting from my HR dollars. How much is HR costing me as a percent of revenue? Is there any payback? If so, how do I measure it?"

"HR has always been siloed in my company, isolated from major aspects of the business, and I don't see any way to change that."

"I always seem to get burned when I bring in a new HR leader or process. We're never able to form a strong working relationship."

If you've asked these questions or had these doubts, then this book is a must read.

In recent years, HR has taken on a dramatic new role as a prime mover of business results. It's not like the old days, where employee management was guided by Frederick Taylor's *The Principles of Scientific Management*. Back then you simply placed people in a production line and put them to work, but HR's role has since gotten a lot more complicated and strategic. HR leaders are now as responsible for contributing to the bottom line as the CFO and other senior members of the leadership team. *A Powerful Team* shows how a business unit that once served a largely tactical role is now at the forefront of strategic planning and execution.

Unfortunately, not enough companies are taking advantage of this new approach. Many organizations are still running HR in the old ways and have not yet embraced the new era we're in.

To find out how CEOs and CHROs are forming powerful teams and developing cutting-edge strategies, we interviewed executives at top companies. Many of these companies have faced significant challenges in recent years, and their executives have had to fundamentally change the culture and direction of their organizations. They have had to improve employee engagement, change mindsets and behavior, and create new business models. They have had to face restructuring challenges posed by mergers, acquisitions, and geographic expansion. The teams of CEOs and HR leaders we interviewed relied on a powerful working relationship to overcome these challenges and create fundamental change.

In talking to them, we sought answers to a host of questions:

--What do CEOs look for in a CHRO and vice versa? What core values create a powerful team?

--How do CEOs and HR leaders complement their skills, strengths, and weaknesses to work together effectively? How can an HR leader help maximize a CEO's leadership potential and capabilities, and vice versa?

--How does HR help create a unified and engaged corporate culture, where shared values and unity of purpose drive performance? How do CEOs and HR chiefs become aligned around common goals?

--How have top CEOs and their HR leaders evolved in how they view HR's role in their organizations?

--What kinds of formative experiences help create world class HR leaders?

--What core values do strategic HR leaders have in common?

--What challenges do female HR leaders face when working with a mostly or all-male senior management team?

--How can HR leaders comfortably and successfully embrace the tension that sometimes exists between business advocacy and employee advocacy?

This book can't provide all the answers to these questions. No single book on HR can do that. Nor does *A Powerful Team* provide all the tactical solutions to the strategic challenges you face. What this book does do is provide you with new ways of thinking about and using HR that you can employ in fine-tuning your own approaches. As a collection of "best practices" and "core values" in using HR strategically, *A Powerful Team* will help you optimize your HR department to successfully address major challenges and opportunities.

As one of the CEOs we interviewed said, "The ultimate measure of HR success is not in tactical things, like involuntary turnover or time to fill positions. I don't want HR to just manage compensation and benefits. HR needs to play an essential role in driving every one of our key results. At the end of the day, our results are all that matter. Therefore, everyone's ultimate measure should be that, and HR is no exception."

We hope *A Powerful Team* helps CEOs and HR leaders discover new ways of viewing their relationship and working together, so they can bring out the best in each other, seize opportunity, meet challenges, and help their employees and companies perform to their fullest potential.

Scott Rosen
Founder and President
The Rosen Group
Cherry Hill, N.J.

David Pinette
Senior Vice President
Challenger, Gray & Christmas, Inc.
Philadelphia, Pa.

John Touey
Principal
Salveson Stetson Group, Inc.
Radnor, Pa.

We're All in It Together

HPE Financial Services
Irv Rothman, President and Chief Executive Officer
Scott Leff, Chief Human Resources Officer

"We operate on a worldwide basis," said Irv Rothman, President and CEO of HPE Financial Services, "and that requires uniting everyone in our community. We have many multinational customers who expect us to deliver consistently on a worldwide basis. If we weren't a cohesive community, that would not be possible. You need the support of HR in order to make that community happen, especially on the organizational design and development side.

"Our entire business is about executing better than the other guy, and in order to do that you've got to first hire the right people and then put them in a position to succeed. Everybody says this, but it's especially true in our business because we don't manufacture anything. For us, it's all about execution.

"There are two very important elements to HR," Irv went on. "The obvious important element is its conventional role, which a lot of HR people are capable of dealing with. The other element, which is perhaps more important, is the organizational development and design side. You can't be a successful HR person in this company unless you can contribute in a way that positively impacts us culturally."

Prior to joining HP, Rothman was President and CEO of Compaq Financial Services (CFS). As leader of the company's 1997 start-up, Irv built CFS into a global business across 43 countries, ultimately achieving

1

$3.4 billion in assets and $1 billion in revenue through joint ventures, acquisitions, and creating new operations. In 2002, Rothman helped oversee the HP/Compaq merger, a deal that married Compaq's global reach with HP's technological prowess and resulted in a state-of-the-art finance and leasing company now producing over $3.5 billion in annual revenue.

Hewlett-Packard Enterprise Financial Services, a wholly owned subsidiary of Hewlett-Packard Enterprise and headquartered in Berkeley Heights, N.J., provides a wide range of technology leasing and financing services to Hewlett-Packard customers in North America, Europe, and Asia. A company of over 1,500 employees and $12.5 billion in assets, it serves government agencies, educational institutions, and businesses of all sizes, offering leasing and financing, asset recovery services, and pre-owned equipment.

"Our team-oriented organization is the backbone of what we do," Irv went on. "We organize our people into self-managed teams. At least a third, if not 40% of our people, are in these teams. If these teams aren't productive, we can't outperform the other guys. And if we can't out-execute the other guys, we're not going to win. So finding the right people is paramount and that's not necessarily just a question of skill level. It also means finding the people who are capable of embracing our operating style. If they're not collaborative, if they're not helping without hesitation, they're not going to fit in here.

"They must have the right mindset to be attracted to and grasp our operational philosophy. It's making sure that they have the capability to work in a self-managed environment, a very collaborative, consensus driven type of organization. We believe in consensus decision-making. And they must be ready not only to work through the current change we're experiencing, but also be ready to navigate change on an ongoing basis."

Irv pointed to the company's "help without hesitation" ethos as a crucial operating principle.

"We're a global organization operating in many different time zones," he said. "It's imperative that our people work together in order to solve

2

the needs of customers, no matter where and when these needs may occur. An employee in Singapore can't say, 'It's seven o'clock at night. My day is over and I really don't want to be bothered.' It doesn't happen that way around here.

"We also do a lot of communicating within the organization, which is very important. We want to make sure our employees have the information they need. Our internal communications group is aligned very tightly with HR, so we can deliver the kind of information that's going to have the right kind of impact."

We asked Irv to talk about his relationship with Scott Leff, CHRO, and what makes them an effective team.

"Scott came here with a financial services background, which is helpful. He was attracted to our operating style and philosophy, and we were attracted by his ability to embrace our approach to business. He's got the kind of personality that enables him to align himself closely with the leadership team. Some of the members of that team have been with me for 31 years, through three different companies—AT&T, Compaq, and HP. That's not an easy crowd to crack into. It can be a little tough to come in from the outside, but Scott fit in immediately.

"We formally meet every other week for forty five minutes or so," Irv said, "and then we have team meetings face-to-face, four or five times a year. We have team meetings by phone in the months that we don't meet face-to-face. I think nothing of wandering down the hall, tapping Scott on the shoulder, and saying, 'I need a couple of minutes.'"

"And vice versa," Scott said. "His door is always open."

Irv and Scott talked to us about HR's role in preparing for rapidly transforming circumstances and events.

"In the business world," Irv said, "everything is in a constant state of change. The market changes, the economic circumstances change, the competitive environment changes. We don't believe in sitting still, so we're constantly in a state of evolution and hopefully improving. If you don't have an effective HR organization to help you through those changes, you will be challenged to succeed."

HPE Financial Services takes a proactive stance in facing the challenges and demands brought about by change, with HR in a lead role.

"There's a learning environment here," Scott said, "and not just for our teams, but for the senior leaders as well. We read books together and hear from pretty important people on topics of significance. This enables us to be forward thinking around our business.

"Irv came to me recently and said, 'I'm really worried about the business.' We had just had a record year and our profits were as high as they've ever been. But Irv was really worried, so we challenged the team to rethink our business. I have never been in a situation where we had so much success, yet were looking to make some substantial changes to ensure we stay on top."

"We believe in productive paranoia," Irv said. "That's not my term, it's from a book by Jim Collins and Morten Hansen called *Great by Choice*. We've adopted it for our own use."

The idea of "productive paranoia" is not for leaders to walk around scared, afraid to make decisions, and suspiciously paranoid about their employees. Rather, Collins and Hansen note that leaders in top companies constantly ask "what if?" They assume that conditions can, and often do, unexpectedly and quickly change. Top business leaders are hypersensitive to these changing conditions, for as Collins and Hansen make clear: "The only mistakes you can learn from are the ones you survive."

One such mistake, Irv noted, is lack of CEO engagement during merger situations.

"The failure rate for M&A transactions in the United States is about 70%," he said. "People overestimate the synergies, they overestimate the time it takes to cost out of their business, they overestimate the strategic advantages. They get 'numbers happy.'

"In my view, the real reason M&A deals fail is because the two companies were taught to beat each other's brains out in the marketplace. All of a sudden they're sitting together and you expect them to sing kumbaya, but that just doesn't happen. In a situation like that, a CEO can't simply delegate things to HR. You have to be an active participant.

I spent a hundred and eighty days on the road after they closed the HP/Compaq deal, talking to people about our operating philosophy and trying to create a strong sense of partnership. There are certain things you simply cannot delegate to HR, because if the CEO is not actively working on the integration and assimilation of an M&A deal, it's going to fail.

"My relationship with the heads of finance, legal, and IT is same as my relationship with Scott," Irv went on. "We're all in this together and we've got to figure it out as a team. We'll either hang together or surely we'll hang separately, as Ben Franklin said."

"As an example of that," Scott added, "a couple of years ago we were trying to identify the values that we want to emphasize throughout the organization, in terms of engagement, branding, and communications. We developed a script for what we really believed in and what best represented the organization. For the next year we asked our CFO to speak at several important employee, manager, and leadership meetings on the topic of culture.

"It wasn't me getting up there or Irv getting up there. We asked the CFO to do it, who is probably the least comfortable person in that role. But he really embraced it and did a great job. That's what we mean by working together as a team."

"One of the reasons why he was so successful," Irv said, summing up, "was because he truly believes in our culture. If you talked to our chief counsel or to our head of information technology, you'd find the same thing. As I said earlier, you need people who believe in your operating style. It may seem obvious, but it isn't typical in a lot of companies."

Creating a Unified Global Company

Houghton International Inc.
Michael J. Shannon, CEO
Kym Johnson, Chief Human Resources Officer

When Kym Johnson interviewed at Houghton International Inc. for the position of Chief Human Resources Officer, she was already planting the seeds for a close relationship with the company's CEO should she be hired. Michael J. Shannon, Houghton's current CEO, held the position of COO when he was part of the team interviewing Johnson.

"As I was interviewing with Houghton," Kym told us, "I knew that Mike would potentially be the CEO, so we engaged in that conversation right during the interview process. I said, 'This is how I want to work with a CEO. How do you want to work with an HR person? Let's start building that rapport now.' I wanted to enter into the relationship with that kind of contract.

"I had learned earlier in my career that absolute trust and candor are necessary," Kym continued. "You must speak the truth. You have to be an HR leader who the CEO can come to and know with confidence that it's a safe place, and that the HR person is going to fully support the CEO. I didn't experience that with a previous CEO. He and I didn't have that rapport."

From the way Kym and Mike interacted during our interview, with such obvious trust and camaraderie, it seemed they had worked together a lot longer than they had. Johnson joined Houghton International as Senior Vice President and Chief Human Resources Officer in June, 2015.

Shannon has been with the company since 2009, and was appointed CEO in January 2016.

Houghton is a global company that manufactures specialty chemicals, oils, and lubricants. The privately held company, founded in 1865, is headquartered in Valley Forge, Pa., and has offices and manufacturing and research facilities in more than 50 locations around the world.

We asked Kym to describe what was at the heart of her working relationship with Mike.

"The relationship with the CEO has to manifest in trust and credibility and integrity," said Kym.

"It helps that Mike operates from a similar value stream. When I mess up or have forgotten something, or don't know something because it isn't within my set of skills, I will go to Mike and say, 'I don't have the answer right now, but if you give me a little time I'll come back to you with the answer.'

"It goes back to that relationship contract. My value system is very much that I need to be authentic and genuine at all times. It relates to integrity, but it's a little bit more than that. I have to be who I am. It's very important for me. If you don't have that relationship, you're going to find yourself being really frustrated as a practitioner. Not because of competency, but because the relationship isn't working.

"Mike and I have had that conversation. He knows where I operate from. That was very much part of the early stages of our relationship, getting to know each other personally and ensuring that the candor was there."

Mike talked about getting beneath the surface as he and Kym spent a lot of time getting to know one another.

"We talked about experiences we encountered, both good and bad, and how we dealt with them," he told us. "Talking frankly about these experiences gives you a better understanding of a person than just saying, 'I believe in motherhood and apple pie.' Great, so does everybody, but what is the other person really like, especially during difficult times?"

Mike had mentioned that he started out as an engineer and has "to see it before he believes it." We were curious if that influenced the way

Kym worked with Mike. Did she have to present information in a more analytical or measurable way in order for Mike to respond?

"It helps that I'm a chemist by background," Kym said. "But I'm also a highly intuitive person. I rely a lot on judgment and prior experience versus just data.

"We're starting to drive business decision-making from more analytical or data-based processes and constructs. Mike likes to see data, but he's also very willing to adapt to my gut feeling about something, based on my experience. He's been pretty open-minded if I don't bring 100% of the data."

"I was a production engineer," Mike pointed out, "and it was always more about people than about design. If you get me 75% of the way there, then the rest is intuition and experience. If you're not going to get me 75% of the way there, then we have a problem because I'm not going to wing it. But I definitely don't need the last bit of detail to make decisions about going forward. You have to trust that the people you've hired have a better feel for a situation because they're closer to it."

Kym cited Dave Ulrich's books on HR management, which focus on shifting the role of HR from administration to strategy, as models she follows for transforming Houghton's HR functions.

"When I came to Houghton," Kym said, "I found our regional HR organizations working in silos, not working on the same things when they needed to. Structure was not following strategy. The structure and design of the organization was reactive, versus really looking at a three to five year business plan and then saying, 'Okay, if this is our strategy, what kind of HR organization do we need to implement it?' We're now making these changes globally. We're building out a three year plan for HR. A big piece of that is building infrastructure, putting in place global processes and systems. The other part of it is making sure that the administrative and tactical approaches we're building in HR relate to our overall strategy and operational goals."

Another challenge facing Mike and Kym was employee engagement, especially after several years of plant closings and workforce reductions.

"Employees felt a bit alienated from management," Mike said, "and we needed to rebuild that trust. The executive team is expendable. The company doesn't need us as much as the company needs its employees. They are the people who run the business. They're the ones that engage with customers. Customers buy from us because of our employees.

"If they think we're figuring out how to make a bunch of money for ourselves while we cut their jobs, that's a terrible environment to work in," he continued. "I don't want a legacy like that. I think we've stemmed the tide. We're spending more time listening to people. We're getting the executive team in front of people. We've started CEO breakfast meetings where there's more engagement with cross sections of employees. In the first round of interactions we didn't discuss much business or strategy. It's just getting to know one another on a personal level and how their jobs help fulfill our mission with customers. "

To make sure that employees were being heard, Houghton developed a communications plan highlighting key aspects of what employees should know, believe, and do. As Kym described it: "What's the knowledge and information they need to have? What are the feelings and the emotions that we want to use to motivate our employees? What are the actions we need employees to take to help us achieve our strategic goals?

"Because of silos in the past, we came up with six enterprise level goals that we're holding ourselves accountable for as an executive committee. Then we're translating those goals through the organization. In every communication we're focusing on at least two or three enterprise goals to really drive the message that we are a unified global company, not a series of international subsidiaries."

Shannon described Houghton's efforts to create global working sessions, where employees throughout its worldwide operations can establish closer working relationships. These in-person sessions were designed to allow participants to practice collaboration and strategy development skills while making progress on critical business goals.

"We've brought together people who didn't have to work together before," Mike told us. "In the past they might have exchanged emails or talked by phone, but they weren't really communicating well. We've cut down some of the barriers that were there, and Kym and her HR team have greased the wheels to make sure that everybody is talking about what needs to be done differently. Those are much easier conversations to have now, rather than communicating only via email or by a phone call in the middle of the night due to a 12-hour time difference."

Kym and her HR team worked closely with the business side of the company in establishing expectations and outcomes for the global working sessions. As Shannon described it: "What's the agenda? What do we want to accomplish? That's where the HR team can really add value, by facilitating those kinds of meetings and achieving the outcomes you're looking for. We couldn't do that without HR's help."

Kym described in more detail her role in these meetings.

"We want people to engage. We don't want it to be overly presentation oriented, which is always possible when you bring business people together. The role that I play is to really drive the outcome we want to achieve. Is it knowledge? A change in behavior? An action we need to take? What do we want to achieve by the end of the meeting? We then take that information and make it actionable going forward."

As a final thought, we asked Mike for the advice he would give to other CEOs who are skeptical about HR's importance in strategic planning.

"I would estimate that only about half of CEOs understand the strategic value of HR. So many CEOs are only about the numbers. I believe that I don't make the numbers alone. For me, it's not a financial exercise, but a people exercise. If you believe you have to communicate and motivate and reward your people to engage them in your strategic vision, but that you don't need an HR expert to help you do that, you're just wrong. You can't do that all by yourself unless you're a small mom and pop company and everybody is a family member.

"Everybody has their particular motivations, but you've got to channel those motivations into what's best for the company. The CEO doesn't have time to do that alone. You've got to team up with a partner who's going to lead you through that process. I've seen lots of other HR professionals who were just focused on the administrative part of it and checking the boxes. But if you don't have everybody working in the same direction under the guidance of HR, the numbers are never going to get there."

Building Accountability and Ownership

Lassonde Pappas and Company
Mark McNeil, President and CEO
Anne Novak, Vice President of Human Resources

A company's CEO and HR leader not only need a close working relationship. They also need to develop multiple strategies to align employees with company objectives. When HR has the same level of accountability for results as the CFO and COO, the results can be striking.

Such is the case with Lassonde Pappas and Company, the U.S. leader in private label beverages. The company, headquartered in Carney's Point, N.J., had a tremendous year in 2015, substantially increasing its EBITDA. For Mark McNeil, President and CEO, and Anne Novak, Vice President of Human Resources, the banner performance was due in some measure to the critical role HR plays in driving performance.

The cornerstone of the company's HR strategy is implementing "The Oz Principle," from the book of the same name by Roger Connors, Tom Smith, and Craig Hickman. The book's core message is that employees will become more invested in their work and perform at a higher level, ensuring not only their own success but everyone else's, when they take personal ownership of their organization's goals and accept responsibility for their performances.

"If people are accountable to themselves and to the organization, they will drive business results," Novak told us. "One of the cornerstones of Oz is that you define your key results and then you connect everyone in the business to them. Having everybody aligned in that way produced extraordinary results in 2015." When Novak says "everybody," she means exactly that: "I can go to our two hundred person plant in North Carolina and say to an operator, 'What's your job?' And he'll say, 'My job is to deliver the five key results.'"

McNeil joined Lassonde Pappas in November 2013, bringing with him 15 years of experience in high visibility retail food and manufacturing environments. Novak joined the company in April 2014, after spending ten years in HR at GE Aviation. In addition to their extensive experience, they brought with them a shared belief in how to utilize HR.

"At GE we organized around concepts," noted Novak. "Here, we organize around results. At GE we viewed HR as the culture keeper. My job at Lassonde goes further—it's to deliver on the five key results. I have the same level of accountability as every other member of our senior leadership team."

McNeil told us: "The ultimate measure of HR success is not in tactical things, like involuntary turnover or time to fill positions. I don't want HR to just manage compensation and benefits. HR needs to play an essential role in driving every one of our key results—sales growth, the employee promoter score, the customer promoter score, and preparing for future acquisitions and future growth. At the end of the day, our results are all that matter. Therefore, everyone's ultimate measure should be that and HR is no exception."

McNeil was not always a firm believer in the power of HR to drive results. In companies where he previously served, HR was led by the CEO and played a non-essential role. That changed during McNeil's tenure at U.S. Foods, where he was Senior VP of Category Management.

"Andy Moss was an incredibly strong HR leader at U.S Foods. He came from a business background. He spoke the language. He had both operational and functional roles, one with the supply chain and one within sales and marketing. I would go to him not only on people issues or comp issues, but on business issues. Andy gave me a new perspective—that HR was there to drive our key results. He was able to add extraordinary value to the company, and Anne does the same thing."

HR's effectiveness at LPC is fueled by McNeil and Novak's close working relationship. While Novak says she definitely had a seat at the table with other CEOs, "Mark is truly the first CEO I have worked with in a long HR career who knows the value of HR unleashed in the business."

That is unusual because most CEOs spend most of their time with sales or sales management or in operations. But Novak knows that Jeffrey Immelt, GE's CEO, spends 20 to 25 business days of the first four months of every year on people issues.

"I won't say that Mark spends quite that much time because we don't have as many people or as many layers in the organization," she said, "but, relatively speaking, he's like Jeff Immelt and Jack Welch in a small business."

McNeil pointed out that "the CEO owns culture—period. If the CEO doesn't have buy-in on the culture, it will never work. But HR owns the execution of that culture. The CEO is the culture coach, and HR is the quarterback executing the culture. I could not execute my culture strategy without HR."

That strategy was needed to address problems in LPC's culture. In 2014, the company's Employee Promoter Score (EPS), measured through an employee survey, was very low. One question asked employees if they would recommend Lassonde Pappas to friends, family, or colleagues as a great place to work. Essentially, EPS puts a number to employee engagement, and the 2014 score demonstrated where LPC had some challenges with regard to employee engagement and communication.

As McNeil recalled, "Historically, LPC was, 'We'll determine what you need to know. Otherwise, keep your head down and just do your job.'"

McNeil and Novak developed a strategy to find out what the problems were and how to best address them. As a start, Novak conducted focus groups at the company's five operating plants.

"I talked to as many people as I could to find out what the numbers meant," she told us. "Why did they vote that way? What was impacting their jobs? I came back with tons of information."

Based on what Novak found out, LPC developed an action plan. "I had ideas and foundational philosophies," said Novak, "and translated those ideas into firm action steps that could be measured and easily communicated."

The action plan was centered on four areas: training and development, working conditions, culture, and performance management. The plan introduced the Oz concept, along with such varied approaches and ideas as new performance management and appraisal tools, summer flex time, enhanced training for every employee, pre-shift meetings, tuition reimbursement, and scholarship programs for dependents of employees. In 2015 the company's Employer Promoter Score increased by a 1,600% margin and the company surpassed its EBITDA target.

"Without Anne's leadership in executing those ideas," McNeil added, "we wouldn't be where we are today."

Full transparency and open communication are now woven into LPC's culture. The company conducts monthly "town hall" meetings with as many employees as possible attending in person. Those who can't attend participate via a webinar. No topic is off limits.

"We read questions at our town hall meetings that most companies would censor," McNeil told us. "We announce departures, resignations, and terminations; we used to go dark on those things. We review the five key results. We take questions and recognize employees. Every month we give away tickets to a Flyers game or another event in Philadelphia. None of these changes would have been possible without HR's leadership role."

As another part of their strategy to boost performance, McNeil and Novak worked closely to upgrade talent, which McNeil is careful to distinguish from recruiting.

"Recruiting is finding a person to fill a particular position in the company," he said. "Talent management is significantly transforming the business through developing and acquiring talent. Anne and I had an alignment that said we needed to significantly upgrade the overall talent in this business over a period of 18 to 24 months, through a combination of exiting underperformers and bringing game-changing talent into the business. This upgrade has had an exponential effect on the business."

In addition, LPC instituted robust individual development programs for every employee, from the janitor in its Seabrook plant to upper management. The "Juiced" program allows employees to attend workshops on the company's core competencies, using technology to drive business results, understanding the company's business model, improving communication, prioritizing work responsibilities, and other topics, to help them grow and perform at their best. LPC's "Juiced Up" program provides accelerated development for employees identified as capable of taking on greater levels of responsibility.

We wondered: what was the nitty-gritty of Mark and Anne's relationship? What were their styles and how did they mesh?

"Not only do I need my leadership to disagree with me," McNeil told us, "I actually encourage it—as long as they have a solution to offer. Don't tell me about something that isn't working without giving me a plan B.

"I think Anne in her own way calls me out more than my other leaders, which is what I need. If she sees me going down a path that isn't fruitful, she lets me know. Anne doesn't do it often, but she does it with conviction and with the best interests of the business in mind. That's because she has a 360-degree view of the business, so the push back is not one-dimensional. She understands the entire business, our customers, and our shareholders."

Anne shed more light on why their relationship works productively.

"In order to properly accept feedback," she said, "you have to trust that the person giving it to you has your best interests at heart. Mark trusts that in me and I trust it in him. When I give him feedback, he understands that it's about me just wanting the best for the business and for him personally. I passionately want him to succeed. I don't give feedback often. I pick my spots and only convey the things that I think are really impactful."

As for advice for other CEOs on how to unleash the talent in HR so it fully impacts the business, McNeil noted that HR leaders have historically been "siloed" within their companies, isolated from major aspects of the company's business by "staying in their lanes."

"Get your HR leader out of the box and engaged in the business. Encourage your HR leader to ask cross functional questions of your leadership team. If the sales guy says something about category management, have the HR person speak up if she doesn't understand what category management is. That has two different purposes. One, the

HR leader is part of the direction of the business. Therefore, she should be aware of our strategic objectives and have a say in whether that's a good use of resources and time. Two, knowing a little about what it takes to be an effective category manager helps shape recruitment for that role. Then the HR leader is not an administrator but a valued member of the leadership team driving key results.

"When you find that person," McNeil continued, "find out where you're aligned. Anne and I were fundamentally aligned on upgrading talent and eliminating cultural negativity. We were aligned on creating a development program for all. We were aligned on open and unfiltered communication. Pick the two or three things that you are fundamentally aligned on, and go execute the hell out of those things."

We asked Anne if she had any last advice for HR leaders on how to work effectively with their CEOs.

"First, it's all about the numbers. Maybe that's a cliché, but it's true. Between my GE experience and my experience at Lassonde, we've found a way to measure HR in every conceivable way.

"Finally, develop a passion for making things simple. It's harder to make things simple than it is to make them complicated. That's a passion both Mark and I share. Glitzy programs with lots of bells and whistles aren't necessarily any more effective than simple, straightforward initiatives."

Facing the Challenges of Change

Citadel Federal Credit Union
Jeff March, President and CEO
Margolit Hillsberg, Senior Vice President and
Chief Human Resources Officer

"We're in an industry that's probably facing more changes than most," said Jeff March, President and CEO of Citadel Federal Credit Union. "My kids never go to a physical branch anymore. When they get a check, they deposit it remotely with their phones.

"As the industry changes and our company expands," Jeff went on, "the HR function might have to grow at a potentially faster pace than other parts of the company. My role is to be out in front of the company by at least a couple of years, trying to get us to where the business is headed. I need to communicate that message to the employee base and then start to transition them into making changes. Humans are creatures of habit. HR is my link to the employee base to say, 'How do we change habits to get to where we want to be? How do we initiate the necessary steps to move people forward and reach our goals?'

"Years ago when we were a much smaller company," Jeff continued, "it was a little easier for the CEO or other people in management to stay involved in employee-facing issues. Now there are too many balls in the air for that to happen. A key to a successful business is to be able to have an HR leader like Margolit, who gets the strategy and understands the business. She can sit at the table with our senior leaders, engage in what we're trying to do, and then go execute on the people side of it."

Citadel is a full-service financial institution chartered as a credit union, and offers a range of products covering deposits, loans, investments, and insurance. Founded in 1937, the company is headquartered in Exton, Pa. Margolit Hillsberg joined the company in 2014 and is Senior Vice President and Chief Human Resources Officer.

With Citadel in the midst of expanding geographically, we asked Margolit how HR is helping the company on that journey, especially in terms of leveraging technology to deliver new services to their members.

"Part of my job," she said, "is to figure out when we might need some new skillsets, new teams, or collaborative efforts that we don't have today. What does that look like and how do we build it out? What's the level of talent we're looking for? What is it going to cost? How do we find the talent and bring them in?

"The second piece that we've been focused on is building a spirit of digital affinity in the organization. That's not to say we haven't been fans of technology. Technology drives almost all of our processes. But technology continues to rapidly evolve and has become transformational for any business, ours included. The HR role is to add new technology training for both new hires and existing employees, so they can gain additional skills and knowledge. As an example, we decided to pilot test Grovo, a cloud-based online training company that offers ninety-second videos on thousands of topics.

"It's very helpful when you're trying to be efficient and want to do things quickly," Margolit added. "You can learn how to set up and use any technology, all in quick ninety-second presentations. That's an example of building digital capability that will multiply throughout the organization on many different topics and with many different sets of employees."

We asked Margolit to describe what she needs from Jeff in order for her HR team to be as effective as it can be.

"There has to be an open and quick line of communication between the CEO and CHRO, and Jeff is very strong on communicating, whether it's a quick email, a quick conversation, or a quick phone call: 'Hey, I was just talking about a particular issue or a particular opportunity. I need you to get involved or I just wanted to let you know.' Jeff and I have that back and forth. We're very focused on making sure that HR is aligned with the business.

"You're able to be more effective that way. He provides great coaching and feedback. That's important for any professional and for me personally."

We asked Jeff to describe the role HR plays in making sure that Citadel's culture remains strong as it expands.

"Right now, I'm doing small group meetings with twelve to fifteen employees at a time throughout different parts of the business. I'll give a business update in the first forty-five minutes, but the real value I get is from listening. I encourage them to interrupt me, to talk to me about what they're seeing, and to share their experiences.

"I'll say to them, 'I'm counting on you, because you know what our culture is. You know what Citadel Class Service is. Don't be afraid to talk to the person next to you if you see something going on that's not quite the way we do things.' I encourage the employees to coach one another. You don't have to say to someone, "Hey, you screwed up and that's wrong.' Instead, you can say, 'I would have done that a little differently, and here's why.' We stress the importance of communication.

"As far as new hires go," Jeff went on, "it's one thing to bring them in and quite another to help them assimilate into your organization. I recently invited three new people from our digital group out to lunch. Of the three, the longest tenured was about a year and half, and another one had been here for just sixty days. I said, 'I love to hear from new people. What are you doing? What do you see?' My goal was to find out how they were assimilating into the organization, because what I don't want to do is create a digital group that isn't a part of Citadel. We have to weave it in. That's one of the issues that Margolit and I have been working on jointly. How do you bring in people with the skills you want but then assimilate them with the rest of the group?"

Integration of new employees is often very dependent on the ability of current employees to accept them. We were curious if that was a challenge from an HR standpoint.

"It could be a challenge," Margolit told us, "but because of the way we've been addressing it, we call it an opportunity. When we were setting up the concept of the digital team, we had a lot of discussions about what we needed here. What was the team going to do? How would they overlap with or mesh with other parts of the organization, whether that's the IT group, our retail delivery groups, or marketing?

"All of those pieces have to interact," she said, "so it required a little bit of organization design, to use the HR technical term, but most of all it was about what we were trying to accomplish from a business strategy perspective. What kinds of structures did we need? What kinds of people? Then going out, finding them, and getting them on-boarded. And we made sure we had people from those other departments involved in the interviewing and decision-making process."

Jeff pointed out another challenge that comes with starting a new company initiative.

"One of the challenges when you start something new is that the people you already have on staff want a shot at it. But there are certain times in the business cycle where you can't wait to develop someone you have. You need to bring in expertise from the outside so you can take leaps instead of baby steps.

"The challenge is to figure out when it's the right time to bring in someone," Jeff said, "because it's tough to say no to the person who wants the job internally. But you have to make that tough decision."

We asked Jeff to describe the key measurements he pays attention to in evaluating the success of HR.

"First and foremost, you have to do blocking and tackling, the basics of benefits and getting people paid timely. Second, I look at the department that she oversees. How's the team? Does she have the right people to get the job done? Are they developing? Do they have the potential to grow?

"What are our turnover and our engagement? Are we keeping the right people? If we have turnover, let's dissect and understand that. If we're losing some people, why did we lose them? Let's talk about that."

And what would Jeff say to other CEOs to help them get the most they can out of their HR team and leader?

"Number one, realize that you're not an HR expert. Don't be afraid to surround yourself with someone who is, who has really good talent and expertise. Look for someone who has high-level experience in the kind of organization you want to be. HR should be one of the key parts of the business strategy. If they're not brought into the strategy, you're going to have a harder time bringing your people along for the wins that you're trying to achieve."

To sum up, we asked Margolit for suggestions on how HR leaders could best engage with their C-teams and increase their effectiveness in working at that level.

"First and foremost, make sure you understand what the business is trying to achieve. What are the goals and the strategy? What are the CEO's long-term goals? What can you do to help execute the strategy and achieve the goals?

"A second piece is to build relationships not just with the CEO," she said, "but with the rest of the senior team and then multiplying that out. Spend time face-to-face with every member of the senior team and with the frontline managers. Do that on a regular basis, and make sure there are open lines of communication in your own team. This gives you a better understanding of the business goals, opportunities that haven't yet been addressed, or things that are falling short and need to be fixed. That way, you can achieve some quick wins.

"Finally, make sure you understand the financials, especially if you're moving into an industry that's new to you. Meet with various leaders throughout the organization and ask them to talk to you about their financials, about the industry, and about the competition. Invest time in getting up to speed as quickly as you can."

Empowering Leadership

Solenis LLC

John E. Panichella, Chief Executive Officer and President
David Nocek, Senior Vice President and
Chief Human Resources Officer

"Talent would be at the top of my list what for what a good HR program looks like," said John Panichella, CEO and President of Solenis LLC. "You need to have a process to understand talent, recruit talent, and build talent—the whole performance management piece. You need to understand how to do that really well. Coaching and development are crucial—how to stretch people, how to give them assignments that make them grow and learn. HR's role is to build effective leaders and give them opportunities to be the best they can be."

Solenis LLC, headquartered in Wilmington, Del., is a manufacturer of specialty chemicals for the pulp, paper, oil and gas, chemical processing, mining, bio-refining, power, and municipal markets. The company's product portfolio includes a broad array of process, functional, and water treatment chemistries, as well as state-of-the-art monitoring and control systems. These technologies are used by its customers to improve operational efficiencies, enhance product quality, protect plant assets, and minimize environmental impact.

The company has been in existence since July, 2014, when Ashland Water Technologies was bought by the private investment firm Clayton, Dubilier & Rice (CD&R) and rebranded as Solenis. We asked John and

Dave Nocek, the company's Senior Vice President and CHRO, to talk about the role of HR in remaking and improving Solenis.

"Every business has a different model," John told us. "As a leader, you assess what model is necessary for your business to succeed. The last business I ran was centered around manufacturing operations and products. You had to have the best products and you needed really strong people in manufacturing technology and R&D. Solenis is a commercial model and that's how this business succeeds. I quickly understood that we had a lot of weakness in the commercial team and that HR had to be remade Because of our model, I knew it was going to be a heavy HR lift to make Solenis better.

"We had to start from the bottom up. This wasn't a small tweak. This wasn't about making a couple of changes. Almost all the functional leaders were new hires. We didn't have any IT employees, very little finance, very little HR. All the corporate functions had to be built. We started with people who had different perspectives.

"As an example, we've replaced 50% of the regional sales directors," John continued. "We've done a lot of HR work around performance management and around leadership. The last business I was in, it was an easier model to manage and change from a leadership perspective. This is much harder. Almost everything we've done to change this business over the last two and half years has been about the people, the culture, and the talent. We needed to change the culture if we were going to really change the results."

We asked John to tell us more about those cultural changes and HR's role in it.

"I think it took Dave six to nine months to work with the leadership team to define what we wanted the culture to be," he said. "Where was it today, what did we want it to be, and what would we have to do to change it? We basically boiled it down to three high level things: people, performance, and results.

"Our fundamental thesis was that if we build the right culture, it will drive how people think about the company. If we create the right environment for employees, if that environment drives how the employees think, if they really believe in what they're doing, they're going to create actions and plans to deliver the kind of results we want. And then we came up with 12 beliefs to really embody and drive the culture.

"To know how well it's working," John went on, "we created an employee survey that's tied in to the 12 cultural elements. We've surveyed the employees twice now for feedback and in nine of the 12 we've made pretty good progress. We're working hard on improving the three areas where we haven't done as well."

Dave Nocek noted that there was initial skepticism about the new initiatives. "I think people might have rolled their eyes," he said, "or thought, yeah, this is nice conversation, but nothing's really going to change. But on the surveys we've been rated very highly on being committed to making changes. The leadership team has spent a lot of time planning and investing in cultural change."

John and Dave both pointed to leadership development, and, in particular, the importance of empowering their functional leaders.

"We don't dictate to our functional leaders how they should work on cultural issues," John told us. "Instead, we challenge them to pick two or three areas where their teams feel we're not yet walking the walk around culture. Their job is to put together focus groups to figure out what we should do to improve those elements.

"I can't tell them what they need to do," John said, "because I'm not smart enough to do that right. I don't know everything that's going to be required to drive the results that we want. The functional leaders are given the responsibility to engage their employees and find out what we need to do better. That's our model.

"I'll give you another example of leadership development. We have consultants or specialists who go out and work with customers. Our objective is to have the best consultants in the world representing us. Well, how do you create the best consultants? You've got to invest in their training. You got to train them not only when times are good, but also when you're going through the bad times. We gave HR a budget to develop a training curriculum and they are required to spend that budget."

John also spoke about cultural changes related to accountability.

"In performance management, one of our key three themes, the culture used to be that if someone's story was good enough, we accepted their story over the results. In other words, someone might say that they had problems in the plant that affected productivity, and if the story was good enough, you could sell your boss on the story.

"That doesn't work for us anymore," he continued. "We changed the way people are evaluated. Take sales, for example. In the past, sales might be one of ten areas where a person was accountable. If you missed your sales target but met your other nine areas of accountability, you were okay. You could get a good rating. We changed that. We said sales are what you are most accountable for. If you miss sales, you can't get a good rating.

"It shocked the organization to know that stories didn't work anymore, that everyone had to have documented results on what they were accountable for. For each of our core beliefs we have action plans that will change the culture."

One of the company's 12 core beliefs is that everyone is responsible for growth and creating a positive customer experience. John told us that he recently visited a plant in Massachusetts where they've increased on-time delivery from 90% to 99%. "This shows that the concepts have filtered down through the company and taken hold," he said.

Yet he acknowledges that changing the culture of Solenis is complicated and remains a work in progress.

"One of our cultural beliefs is that we value diversity as a competitive advantage," he said. "Yet when we look at some of our populations, we aren't overly diverse. The only way we can change that is to change the way we hire. Dave and I talk about that a lot. We expanded the slate of people we interview for any position. For every opening, we strive to have a diverse group of candidates. As a result, we've greatly increased diversity in our hiring. In 2016, 40% of new hires were from diverse groups."

To sum up, we asked John and Dave to talk about what makes them a good team and their thoughts on what makes an effective HR leader.

"I use Dave as a sounding board for everything," John said. "What do we need to do differently, what do we need to do smarter, and what are we not doing so well? Dave helps me think about how to make the organization better. He knows as much as I do.

"Payroll and benefits are obviously important to the organization," he went on, "but when you think of their value in making a business better, it's pretty limited. I want an HR expert who knows how to think about making the business better."

"It's important to be aligned," Dave added. "John assesses the organization similarly to the way I do. We look at the problems, the issues, and the challenges in the same way. An effective HR leader has to go beyond just doing the HR fundamentals.

"The HR operational stuff, the blocking and tackling, is secondary compared to the focus on trying to improve the business," he said. "It almost has to be. I have group leaders who handle the operational side of HR, because of the ten questions John asks me every day, none of them are related to the operational side of HR. An effective HR leader has to be able to assess and diagnose the organization, and then solve the culture problems, the business problems, and the problems on the CEO's plate."

Building and Implementing a Strategic HR System

NFI Industries
Sid Brown, CEO
Nancy Stefanowicz, Senior Vice President, Human Resources

"HR didn't really exist in our organization 17 or 18 years ago," said Sid Brown, the CEO of NFI Industries. "The role of HR in the past was strictly administrative, more tactical than strategic. We needed a more seasoned HR executive who could help us not just hire people, but think through the strategy of hiring people and the strategy of what the organizational structure might look like in the future. Then Nancy joined the organization 10 years ago and helped us start that thinking process."

Nancy Stefanowicz is Senior VP, Human Resources at NFI, and Sid went on to tell us about the impact she's had on the company.

"During a 10-year period NFI grew about six times in size," Sid pointed out, "and we needed to attract and retain the very best talent to handle that growth. Identifying the skill sets needed, defining where they would fit into the organization, and how the organization can adapt change are all areas where I utilized Nancy to help us think these things through."

NFI Industries, headquartered in Cherry Hill, N.J., has been family owned and operated since 1932. When Sid Brown and his brothers first joined the company in the early 1980s, it focused mainly on over-the-road trucking services. The company has since evolved to provide a range of supply chain services, including dedicated transportation, warehousing, intermodal, brokerage, and transportation management.

"Ten years ago there was nothing," Nancy told us, describing how HR has evolved in the company. "There was a policy manual in a big red binder. We knew where people worked and how much money they made, but not much else. We had no compensation plans. We had no market data. We had no bonus plans. We had to build the infrastructure for all of that. We didn't have a service center, a benefits hotline, or a benefits team. We didn't have partners for outsourcing, so the first five years were about building an HR system and infrastructure, and then partnering with the businesses to understand their needs. We had to formalize a strategy and execute it.

"We rolled out our mission, vision, and values," Nancy went on, "and then we had to go to our people and say, 'What works and what doesn't work?' We learned where we had some gaps, and we created actions plans for the next couple of years to address people's needs. We really wanted HR to be seen as something that could have a positive impact on the organization, that did what they said they were going to do, and that helped the organization transform into a place that people wanted to be, because we didn't have that reputation when I came in ten years ago."

Nancy was fortunate to be partnered with a CEO who understood HR's value.

"The CEO sets the stage for HR's ability to have influence within the organization," she said, "and I'll say that I've been blessed both times that I've worked for CEOs, both in my last life at Hess and in this life at NFI. I've truly has the pleasure of working with enlightened CEOs who believed in the value of HR. The first CEO I worked with knew the value because he had seen it before. I was brought in to help with acquisitions and grow the company, so it was a roadmap of where HR could help take the company."

We asked Sid how he measures the value of HR.

"There are two areas where a CEO says, 'Damn, why am I spending this much?'" he said. "One of them is IT. Why have we had so many IT people? What's my payback here? Another one is HR. How much is HR costing me as a percent of revenue? Because you look at HR and you say, 'Okay, we're spending this, but what's the payback, and how do you measure the payback?'

"What we measure is our retention of employees, turnover of employees, and what it costs to onboard an employee. We look at how many people we have to recruit from the outside versus how much talent we can recruit internally. We made a huge transition about six years ago, where we went to a new HRIS system called UltiPro. It was about streamlining the process, trying to make it paperless and easy for employees. We wouldn't have been able to grow the way we did if we didn't have the systems in place.

"And then five years ago we set up what's almost an internal MBA program for high potential employees. We had 16 people go through the program five years ago, and 13 of those people are now in leadership positions with us. We were able to give them the ability to grow and to work in different parts of the company. If you can't give your people new opportunities you lose them, especially your top performers. We want NFI to be a place people want to work, and after ten years we're on the list of the top places to work in the Philly area."

Nancy told us more about how HR has helped drive the business numbers.

"Hiring 3,100 people, first of all, had a huge bottom line impact," she said. "When we first took over driver recruiting, we cut a couple of million dollars out of the advertising budget immediately. We put in a system to be able to track retention, and turnover has dropped from 105% to about 30% now. We always measure things like reductions in advertising spent, renegotiating contracts, and unemployment, so we look to have revenue drivers wherever we can. And then we look to bring in value by keeping our overhead pretty stable while decreasing the turnover rate."

Sid told us more about Nancy's value, particularly during times of rapid change.

"When a company grows as quickly as we did, the challenge for a CEO is whether he can mentally handle it. One of the fundamental things that Nancy provides, and what a good HR partner should provide, is being a sounding board. A lot of times we don't agree on a course of action. That's okay, because we can agree to disagree, but mostly we are very aligned. With all the folks that report to me, we're not always going to agree, but they need to support me even if they disagree because the organization will not function otherwise. I trust my senior management team and equip them to run the areas they are experts in.

"I want to hire the strongest and most talented team I can, and I'm not fearful about hiring people smarter than me. HR can really help CEOs surround themselves with people who complement their weaknesses and who bring their own strengths to the organization."

"Sid totally supports HR," Nancy added. "Like he said, we don't always agree, but I'll tell you that he's always open to hearing the other side. I present everything that I think needs to be accomplished in a business case and we'll talk about it. The vast majority of the time I'll get support from him because we've already gotten some of those wins."

In addition to having people disagree with him, Sid also pointed out the value of "disruptors" in any business.

"You want disruptors in your organization—people who aren't necessarily of the same culture or the same thinking. People don't like disruptors, but you need them and you've got to figure out if your organization is ready for them. We brought in a fellow four a half years ago, and when he first arrived most people were scared to death of him because of his mannerisms, his abrasiveness, and his aggressiveness. He was a disruptor, but he's done a marvelous job in growing one of our divisions from almost nothing to $150 million. Because of his abrasive nature, this individual had to be coached and counseled along the way. You've got to find those kinds of balances and HR can help you figure that out."

We were curious about Nancy's initial ability to integrate into the executive team, especially since a trucking company is a very male environment and Nancy is the only top female executive in NFI.

"Do you want the truth? Ten years ago when I joined the executive team, I cried a lot. It was a 100% different culture. People were allowed to compete against one another, so when I came in and tried to offer suggestions or a best practice, it was not met with open arms. We went for some quick wins, and Sid saw that it was meaningful, and we realized that some of the folks on the leadership team might not have been the right ones.

"Our organization has totally changed, but I think the biggest thing that has gained respect for HR was letting the business units know we weren't there to tell them what to do. We were there to understand their business and to see how human capital could help them evolve. Once they saw lower turnover, an improved system, and tools that enabled them to get their jobs done in a collaborative way, from there it was easy. HR used to the last phone call. We weren't invited to meetings. Now we're probably the first phone call, almost always. That's a big evolution.

"Today I have a unique and individual relationship with everyone on the executive team. I'm kind of the go-to person, if it's about how to cross something to another division, or how to break down a silo, or whether it's a problem within an individual business unit or with a customer. I don't think there's anybody on the executive team that doesn't partner with me in most of their business challenges."

To sum up, we asked Nancy to describe the greatest strengths of her HR team.

"Our HR team is exceptional for the amount of work that they can accomplish with lean teams. Even though we're a group of almost 50 strong, half of those are recruiters and the other half is doing all of the functions, so that's a pretty lean team that gets a tremendous amount of work done. I think they're exceptional because they know the business just as well as the business partners do. I think they're exceptional because they're willing to do whatever it takes, and I would say they're exceptional because they're not afraid to push back when appropriate.

"I can do compliance all day long," she went on. "I know the laws, I know FLSA, and I know what we need to do to get the job done. But I'm much more interested and better equipped to influence business decisions, to see where the organization is going, and to see what we need from a human capital perspective to support our growth and development. If you asked the employees of NFI, 'What is HR?', they wouldn't say, 'The 401K Administrators.' They're going to say, 'The people that help us grow the business.'"

Earning a Seat at the Table

PMA Companies
Vincent T. Donnelly, President and CEO
Andrew J. McGill, Senior Vice President, Human Resources
and Facilities Management

For Andrew J. McGill, being a successful HR leader means contributing something to the company that goes beyond the norm of what's traditionally expected.

"HR people often say, 'I should have a seat at the table because I'm in charge of HR and HR is an important function.' I never say those words. If I haven't earned my seat at the table, I'm not asking for it. My position alone doesn't get me there," said McGill, who serves as Senior Vice President, Human Resources and Facilities Management, at PMA Companies.

"You've got to come to the table with something special," he went on. "You need to take a step back and ask, 'What can I do or bring to the table that complements the abilities of the CEO? What can I add of value?' A lot of people are giving advice to the CEO, but you have to find a way to add value to the CEO's thought processes so he or she reaches out and says, 'I want your thoughts on this.'

"Some HR people are not as focused on that kind of contribution for a variety of reasons," McGill continued. "Perhaps it's outside of their traditional skill set. But you can't be a successful HR leader unless you have that type of relationship with your CEO or something close to it. And don't wait to be invited to that relationship—you have to make it happen."

McGill has forged just that kind of relationship with Vincent T. Donnelly, President and CEO of PMA Companies. The two have worked together for ten years and have developed a strong vision of how HR should be fully integrated into the company. This vision is especially important as PMA, which specializes in workers' compensation and property and casualty insurance, and is headquartered in Blue Bell, Pa., expands geographically.

"As we venture into new areas," Donnelly said, "how do we make sure that our culture doesn't get off track? In our geographic expansion, particularly into the Midwest, we've added more than 60 people, or 5% of the company's workforce. Our Connecticut operation doubled in size, in terms of volume and profits and people. We're going into states where we've not been before and we're hiring people that don't know us as well. They're coming from multiple companies with different cultures, and our ongoing challenge in the interview and onboarding process is to acculturate them to the way we do things. I think our culture remains very strong as we grow because of the role played by Andy and his people."

Donnelly cited the integration of HR into all aspects of the business in explaining what makes McGill and his staff so effective.

"If Andy left tomorrow," Donnelly told us, "I'd search for someone who didn't want to be just an HR professional. Compliance and processing and all those things are certainly important to get done, but I'd look for somebody who wanted to understand the business as thoroughly as Andy does because that makes a tremendous difference for me. It also makes a tremendous difference for the other senior executives in the company, who benefit from the HR person's advice, suggestions, and insights.

"We're clearly getting more out of human resources today, not only from Andy, but from the staff he's built," Donnelly went on. "His views filter through the staff and he challenges them to be engaged with the business. They've realized that, in order to be effective, they have to develop relationships with their colleagues throughout the different parts of the organization. I don't think that existed before. I realize more than ever how that makes a tremendous difference."

McGill says that he and Donnelly had to work on their relationship. Although McGill had been a customer of PMA before he joined it, he didn't have a fully formed perspective on the inner workings of an insurance company.

"The relationship and trust that Vince and I have today is not the same as in our first couple of years. It took effort and work on both our parts. At times I felt I couldn't provide the best advice to him based on gaps in my knowledge. I worked very hard early on to overcome that gap. One of the things that made it easy is that Vince is very open to mentoring people. If you're working to improve yourself to help the company, he's very willing to invest in you, which is different from other CEOs I've worked with and known."

Donnelly added: "Andy has the ability to bring clarity to issues and provide an unvarnished view. At our strategy meetings, he asks good probing questions. Sometimes his colleagues might wonder why he's asking those questions. That's because it's not textbook HR he's giving me. He's providing HR in the context of underwriting or an organizational issue. He understands the nuances of the business and the people we have. I don't always agree with him and don't always take his advice, but he gets me to think differently and influences my decision making."

Each company has its own definition of culture. We asked Donnelly and McGill to define what it means at PMA.

"I'll answer that in two parts," Donnelly said. "First, we've had the same values over the twenty years that I've been CEO—passion, teamwork, professionalism in how we treat each other inside and outside the organization, accountability, and execution. You'll see those values listed in our lobby and in every office throughout the company.

"Second, I tell everybody that they make a difference, either positive or negative, every single day. I also tell them that they're not going to make a positive difference every day. I know I don't. Some days I'm not at my best. But hopefully we're having more positive days than not so positive.

"Andy and I joke some days that if it wasn't for the people, the job would be easy, but without the people, there'd be no job. We want to grow as much as we can but you've got to have the right people. It's really important for that to be our top priority in recruiting. Someone may have a great resume, have the right skill sets, and so forth, but it's up to Andy and HR to determine if that person fits with the culture."

"Underlying that strategy," McGill added, "is a phrase you've probably heard: if you love what you do, you never work a day in your life. We have that built into our approach, whether someone works for us already or that person is thinking about joining us. We want to know what really drives their passion and makes them happy during the course of the day.

"They need the technical skills to do the job and they have to fit into our culture," McGill continued, "but we want to take that to the next level and put them in a position where they really like what they do. No one likes everything about a job but if on balance they really like what they do, we're unlocking their creativity, their passion, and their energy. We're giving ourselves the best chance of getting everything we can from that person."

If there's anything PMA does that's unique, Donnelly and McGill said it's probably the amount of energy they put into matching people with jobs they love. This approach is integrated into PMA's recruitment process, performance management process, and compensation program. One of the ongoing dilemmas that companies face is having a really good performer who can only grow in his or her career through a management track. That person may not be cut out to be a manager or want to be a manager, but it's the only next step open to them.

"We've built into our compensation program a track for management and a track for individual performers," said McGill, "so that people are not encumbered by a structure that doesn't allow them to continue to progress in their careers. It's putting our money where our mouth is in terms of saying we really want people to love what they do."

One of the more exciting roles that HR plays at PMA is in predictive analysis. HR has a compliance role and a processing role, and because of the processing responsibility it owns a lot of data. Data has been used, historically, as a retrospective tool to demonstrate what's happened in the past. Over the last few years PMA has been using its HR data to do more of the predictive work.

"We use to inform our thinking about what we're going to do next," McGill said. "As an example, I'm also in charge of facilities for the company. Part of my job is finding the buildings we're going to work in as we expand geographically. Where will we located? Where will we have the most impact?

"Again, we go back to data. We have access to enormous amounts of information about our operation and what's going on. What I'm able to bring to the table is employment trends for particular marketplaces and data on current employees who have experience in that marketplace. Using the data that's available to us informs our thinking about where we should go next."

We asked Donnelly if there were any defining moments when the company's culture was challenged and what role HR played in addressing the situation.

"In 2010 we sold the company and became a subsidiary of Old Republic International. Once we announced that, a lot of people were concerned about their jobs and what that meant for our culture. That required a lot of attention from me, but also from Andy and his folks. We came through that situation with very little turnover. Andy led our communication effort so there were no false assumptions about what our plans were. We both traveled to a lot of the field offices and marshaled the troops, so to speak.

"I wouldn't say it was a crisis, but it certainly was a challenge because it potentially threatened the fabric of the organization. People could have panicked and left, but thanks to Andy's efforts they stayed calm and we got through that change very well. We spend a lot of time being out front and being as transparent as we can."

As a final question, we asked Andy McGill to describe the values and traits he looks for in building his HR teams.

"An open mindedness around how HR is to be delivered. There's an axiom that an old boss of mine told me years ago: 'Rule number one in good employer relations is to get the paycheck right.' That stuck with me—your fundamentals and your execution have to be flawless. You've got to design processes to eliminate human error to the best extent you can.

"But that's not the end of the day for HR. Let's become advisors and consultants. Some people believe HR shouldn't be involved or can't be helpful in those things. I need people on my team who are willing to overcome that bias by demonstrating that they're adding a value in a different way. Come to the table with something of value that other people haven't seen."

Using HR to Grow the Business

Publicis Touchpoint Solutions
Michelle Keefe, President and CEO
Andrew Adams, Chief Talent Officer

Although she's now a firm believer in the value of HR as an equal partner in driving company performance, Michelle Keefe, President and CEO of Publicis Touchpoint Solutions, said she didn't always feel that way.

"I started my career in field leadership, so my exposure to HR had been limited to the onboarding process, or talking to HR whenever someone had a performance issue or was in trouble in some way," said Keefe, who has now led Touchpoint for almost five years. Headquartered in Yardley, Pa., Touchpoint designs and implements customized healthcare sales, service, and communications teams. It is a division of Publicis Health, the largest health-oriented agency network in the world.

"Like most people, I didn't see the point of talking to HR about how to grow the business," Keefe continued. "My view changed when I took on a leadership role in operations and headquarters. That's when I saw the value of HR in providing insights that would get the best business results. I'm a big believer that recruiting and retaining the right talent and properly engaging that talent directly correlates with better business performance. There's no question that a highly engaged workforce leads to greater productivity. Marrying positive business outcomes with great organizational outcomes is precisely what an excellent HR partner facilitates."

Keefe's excellent HR partner is Andrew Adams, Chief Talent Officer of Publicis Health. Adams said he values an "absolutely transparent and candid relationship" with his CEO.

"I've never been shy about providing feedback to executive leadership," Adams told us, "and I always welcome feedback about myself. But the relationship between a business leader and an HR leader is unique. Michelle and I have conversations that she's likely not having with anyone else, including our CFO, who is her next closest relationship in running the business. From early on, I wasn't shy about sharing my opinions about what I was observing, whether in the context of the leadership team or one-on-one with Michelle.

"Once we established that our relationship was based on honesty and candid feedback," Adams continued, "the leadership team could see that our shared agenda is entirely about the success of the organization and not about ego. I want to make sure that I'm maximizing the CEO's leadership capability and leadership potential. That's my sole interest in that relationship."

Keefe admitted that she wasn't always receptive to the kind of honest feedback that Adams described.

"Before I met Andrew," Keefe said, "it wasn't my strength to hear out everybody before I made a decision. Most CEOs don't get to hear HR's views from a business perspective. Now everybody gets their day in the sun to say what they want to say.

"A CEO has to be nimble, quick, and decisive," she added, "but sometimes people are very focused on the speed of the decisions and don't really vet them the way they should. Andrew and other HR leaders I've worked with have really helped me think through the appropriate level of risk we should take to get to a desired result. What could derail this strategy versus that strategy? What am I not seeing? That's what our business partnership looks like.

"Andrew and I talk a lot about how we're going to grow the business," Keefe went on. "We have an amazing recruiting engine that helps all of our customers. How do we take the capability that we have—that everyone recognizes us for—and evolve it even further? What kind of investments do we need to make to create an even more profitable business? That's the game changer we're looking for.

"Everyone on the leadership team sees Andrew as a business partner," Keefe explained. "He's very clear on my overall strategic vision and what we're trying to accomplish from a talent perspective. Whenever I present anything, I present it both as a business opportunity and a people opportunity. If we put the right people in place, we will drive results. You can have the greatest C-suite in the world, but it's the people in the trenches doing the hard work and heavy lifting who understand the heart and soul of the organization."

Adams feels fortunate to work with a CEO who reinforces how the HR team should partner with the business team. "Michelle always makes sure to get HR involved, whether there's a need for more training or more resources, or if we're not acting quickly enough in certain situations. She doesn't just say that HR should work with the business team. She models it in how she interacts with the team and her direct reports."

We asked Adams to describe Touchpoint's HR strategy and how it is integrated into the organization to drive results.

"Our HR strategy is, first and foremost, performance," Adams said. "We are business leaders thinking about revenue, margin, and growth. When I sit down with my leadership team, they know that I'm going to start with where we are in terms of margin. Are we running profitably? Are we having trouble spots that we need to talk about? It means showing up as a business leader. The strategic and the operational are two sides of the same coin. The traditional HR stuff is only important if we have a successful and healthy business.

"The heads of the HR team, the talent acquisition team, and HR operations are each functional experts in their own right, but they must partner with our business leaders to drive success. They're client facing and senior leadership team facing, every one of them. When I hired them, I said, 'Your counterpart is not me or your peers. Your counterpart is the CFO, the head of operations. Your counterpart is the head of the contact center and the head of client services. Those are the people you need to partner with.'"

Adams said the second part of the company's HR strategy is engagement. Like many companies, Touchpoint conducts an engagement survey to make sure its employees have the instructions, tools, and resources to do their jobs. "They have an opportunity to provide feedback on what they think is going well or not going well, and on where they need help," Adams said. "The feedback we receive is heard, assimilated, and acted on." Over the past four years, engagement at Touchpoint has improved from 71% to 82%, and the commitment by everyone in the organization and not just the leadership team is to continue that trend over the next four years.

The third focus is talent management. "We're a performance culture," Adams told us. "When someone starts with this company, the first thing he or she does is work with their manager to establish and agree on their objectives, which are linked to the five overall objectives of the leadership team. In every single leadership team meeting, talent management is on the agenda. It's part of our culture and conversations. We have an annual all-day offsite meeting where each executive team member reviews a number of people in the organization. We do a professional development plan on each person that's being reviewed, and we talk about succession plans and where we can move people who are ready for new positions in the organization."

Keefe told us that Touchpoint has done an excellent job with mobility— getting people new opportunities across the entire organization. "When people get new cross-functional experiences, that helps to drive deeper engagement, which in turn drives productivity." Over the last seven years, Keefe said, the company has invested in growing its talent capability, resulting in an annual compound growth rate of about 19%.

Adams added, "We've taken people who are hitting on all cylinders, fully succeeding in their current roles, and put them into new assignments because we want to stretch them. We're growing great general managers and leadership capacity within the organization when we do that. They can go back to their old positions, but now with a new set of skills as well as capabilities in an additional functional area."

This kind of talent management, Adams told us, is critical to the performance pillar and the engagement pillar: "People are inevitably very engaged when they see we're as invested in their development as they are."

A key competency that Touchpoint looks for in hiring is the ability to "think across the organization."

As Adams said, "We're looking for people who understand what we call 'enterprise thinking' or 'enterprise leadership.' We look for people who will think widely, with good peripheral vision across the business. They have their functional expertise down, for sure, but they know how to think cross-functionally and consider inter-dependencies—how their decisions will impact the rest of the organization."

High on the list of HR's values at Touchpoint is its ability to listen to people within the organization. Keefe talked about the importance of going beyond the feedback that employees traditionally provide.

"As much as you try to create an environment where providing feedback doesn't result in negative consequences, some people simply don't believe that no matter what's said or done. Our HR team is great at listening to the little bit of noise beneath the surface. They're able to get at those underlying things that people don't necessarily have the guts to say as directly as you'd want them to say and, as a result, we're able to tackle things before they become problems. Nothing ever spreads like wildfire because HR is picking up on it pretty quickly and proactively addressing it."

Asked to sum up the importance of HR to Touchpoint, Keefe returned to HR's value in strategic planning.

"You need to be attached at the hip with your head of HR, talking through what you can do to motivate your folks to do their best work, how to tie them to the overall strategy of the organization, and to make sure they understand their critical importance to the overall growth objectives of the organization. Investing in that relationship with your head of HR is what gets you through the tough years, because anybody who says that their business does well 24/7 is selling you a bridge in Brooklyn.

"When I conduct our company's town hall meeting," Keefe concluded, "the first thing I say is, 'The reason we've been so successful is because our people are resilient, they're committed, and they're constantly focused on being the best they can be.' And you can't do that without having a partner in HR."

The True Role of HR is Helping Leaders to Lead

Rentokil North America

John Myers, CEO
Scott Cook, Chief Human Resources Officer

"When you're new in business, you view HR through three lenses—hiring, benefits, and payroll," said John Myers, CEO of Rentokil North America, explaining how his conception of HR has changed over the years. "Early in my career, that was how I saw HR—you went to them when you wanted to change a dependent or when your paycheck wasn't right.

"As you start to mature as a leader, you realize that the HR team can play different roles. Of course the paperwork has to be done, all the tactical stuff, but your view of HR becomes much more strategic."

Rentokil North America, headquartered in Reading, Pa., is one of the leading full-service pest control companies in the U.S., serving both residential and commercial customers. Rentokil North America is also a market leader in its interior landscaping and brand protection businesses. Scott Cook is the company's CHRO and has been with the company for three and a half years.

"When I first met John, we talked for two hours but might have spent ten minutes on HR," Scott said. "We talked about business and growth and how you measure success. We discussed the value proposition for colleagues, and what they were trying to build and achieve as a company."

"We were a homegrown business with homegrown ideas," Myers added. "Scott came in with business acumen and a very broad variety of experiences, which allows him to have a more strategic view of the world."

Rentokil North America is in the midst of growing through acquisitions. The company now has over 7,000 employees working in over 250 locations in the U.S., as well as Canada, Mexico, Central America, Puerto Rico, and the Dominican Republic.

"We're growing from a small, geographically localized business to a large, multi-national, and very dispersed business," Myers told us. "A business that was $250 million when we took it over in 2008 is going to be a $1 billion business in 2017."

We asked Myers to tell us about HR's role during the company's recent mergers.

"Scott is doing his job on the due diligence side," John said, "to make sure we understand what we're buying. *Harvard Business Review* has identified that only a very, very small percentage of acquisitions actually deliver on the business base. The value that was supposed to be created is usually very small.

"That means one of two things—either the business case was faulty, or the integration of the businesses was faulty. I think it's the latter. To successfully integrate businesses, you need two elements. The first is following a set of processes that will deliver the business case, and the second is winning over the hearts and minds of the people you've acquired so they're helping you to deliver on that business case. That's where HR becomes really key.

"Once we've done the acquisition," Myers went on, "Scott is usually very close to the guys on the ground to ensure that they understand where we're headed with the integration of the businesses. Sometimes it's tough news, but we do that at industry or above industry standards."

Myers also told us about a second important role that Scott plays, as a confidante to the CEO and the organization as a whole

"Being a CEO is a very lonely job," John told us. "You can talk about 50% of what you want to talk about, but the other 50% you have to hold in. You worry about how you're performing, whether the board is happy, whether the employees are happy. I can talk to Scott about these things, and as a result I'm healthier and also more confident as a leader.

"Second, Scott is also a confidante to the organization. There are times when people don't want to give me some bad news, so they'll go through Scott, who will talk to me about how things are going. Sometimes I'll say to him, 'Look, I'm really worried about this colleague. I think it could come from me, but it might be better if it came from you, so they have a chance to feel like it's off the record.' Scott's built up enough trust within the organization that the stories he hears won't be repeated, and he also knows how to take things in context. If someone's just having a bad day and unloads on him, Scott knows he doesn't have to share that with me.

"In turn, I'm able to share my thoughts with him about people or decisions. Sometimes I say, 'Look, I'm thinking about this, what's your view?' I use him as a sounding board before I pull the trigger on an idea. As a result, the quality of my decisions has improved."

We asked Scott to reflect on how his relationship with CEOs has evolved over the years and the roles he's played.

"The relationship works the best is when there's recognition of the need for different perspectives. The old model the CEO is the 'my way' type of person where everybody has to get onboard behind him.

"I was fortunate to work with a really good CEO earlier in my career. He was committed to learning new ideas and seeking feedback. John is the same way. I've seen him grow and learn and question. The traditional role of the 'great man' theory of leader has been replaced with people who are authentic, transparent, and honest about who they are. I think that's most productive.

"One of the things John often discusses with our leaders," Scott said, "is the humility of knowing that one person doesn't have all the answers and that we need other people to help us think things through together. The senior leaders who are most comfortable in their skins have the authenticity, transparency, and humility to say there's no single answer. Rather, let's build this together.

"I remember having an executive team meeting to talk about strategy after one of our crisis moments in the company," Cook recalled. "John started off the meeting saying, 'Guys, I'm not sure I had this 100% right, so nothing is off the table.' That was a seminal moment that really changed how the executive team worked together. It changed the tone of our relationship.

"When we're in an acquisition situation, we try to talk about humility. We're not here to conquer you. We bought you for a reason and it's not just the asset turn. We bought you because there are things you know that we don't. How do we figure it out together?

"My advice for the CEO," Scott summed up, "is to marry authenticity, transparency and, humility, while still retaining the hard-edged business skills that you need. The CEOs who are the most successful are the ones who have managed to do that."

We asked Scott about his advice for other HR leaders on how to make strategic contributions to their companies.

"First, learn how to make the trains run on time. Do that flawlessly, and you will earn the right to trade up into the game a little more. Today, John and I probably spend 20% of our time together talking about HR-related matters. If you prove that you can keep the trains running on time, there's an opportunity to have an even greater impact. The fact that we were buying businesses at the rate of one a month gave me a lot of credibility in this organization for handling crisis or difficult situations, and I think that accelerated my ability to contribute."

We asked Scott what influenced his current view of HR.

"If I go back to how I grew up in HR, I worked for a man named Dick Morrisey right out of grad school. He was a former GE guy who has since passed on. There's a ton of folks in the Philly community that have traced themselves back to Dick in some way, shape, or form.

"Early on, Dick would look for people who knew about business and who understood the dynamics of organizations, or OD sensibilities as he called them, and put them in HR roles. That started to shape my understanding of HR from a business perspective. What are the drivers of cost? What are the drivers of revenue? How do you make money in the business? How do decisions get made? How does work get done?

"Beyond that, I began to understand the true role of HR," Scott said. "First and foremost, it's to help leaders lead. Not to lead on their behalf, but to help make sure that leaders are enabled. That can be coaching or training, or sometimes it's pushing and pulling. But sound HR practices should create the structures that help leaders lead. If you don't have sound HR and people practices, you don't get to play in any of those other realms.

"Another piece centers on the renewal of the organization. That's bringing people in, helping them develop and go through their lifecycle here, and also helping people leave well, if that turns out to be the case. Sometimes leaving well doesn't necessarily mean on their terms, but it can still end well. You're bringing people in, you're helping them to be the best they can be while they're here, and you're renewing and refreshing the organization.

"The final piece is really around culture. You guard the culture by making sure that your decisions, from a business standpoint and a people standpoint, are consistent with what you want to be."

One of the challenges that the company faces is turnover.

"In a field-based business like we are," Cook said, "you know during the course of a year you're going to experience significant turnover. But we don't want to wait until there's an opening to fill a position. We've engaged in workforce planning with operations, by getting managers to step up as partners in the hiring process. Instead of managing just to a budgeted head count number, they bring in new people a bit early. They might have a couple of weeks of overlap, but they also know within a reasonable certainty when people are going to turn over.

"Last year, John challenged the executive team: 'There's a lot of churn in the organization. We need to spend more time listening and a little less time telling.' The executive team committed to visiting a number of locations over the course of three or four months, to spend some time in the coffee room just listening to what colleagues had to say. This approach has impacted the engagement of our colleagues. We've learned a lot and I think it's helped drive growth and profitability.

"Every business says they value colleagues," Scott concluded, "but what really happens when you put the colleague in the center? You're willing to listen, not just tell. You're willing to pay at or above average benefits. You're willing to invest in training and development in nontraditional ways. You invest in putting them in the best position to make good choices for our customers. All of those things together help eat away at turnover."

John Myers said that he looked for Scott and HR "to do the right thing for our colleagues. How do we have better wellness programs or other programs that have a longer term payout but help our people today? I want to create a culture of caring in the organization. We offered college scholarships this year for employees, their spouses, and their dependents. I want our employees to be in a position to learn and grow. That's the more creative side that I ask of HR."

In concluding the interview, we asked Myers to offer advice to CEOs about how to make a strong partnership with their HR teams and leaders.

"Some CEOs are totally dependent on their CFOs, and I get that," John said. "They're probably more comfortable with the numbers side of the business, and who knows the numbers better than the CFO? There might be industries where that makes 100% sense, but I would suggest that in most businesses you're better off having a close relationship with the head of HR. Scott and I talk first thing every morning for 15 minutes about our agenda. Every day, we know we're going to have that conversation.

"One of the things that I've realized over the years is that most businesses have the same technology and the same products. There are nuances to be sure, but the main difference between businesses is not the 'what,' but the 'who.' Most businesses base their success on the quality of the people they have and the engagement of those people. And if that's the case, how can you accomplish your goals without HR playing a strategic role?"

Developing the Right Talent to Capitalize on Opportunities

Teleflex

Benson Smith, Chairman and CEO
Cam Hicks, Vice President, Global Human Resources and
Employee Communication

Cam Hicks was upfront with us when we asked him why he joined Teleflex Inc. in 2013 as its HR chief.

"If there isn't a shared philosophy around talent, if there isn't a high level of mutual respect, it would be very unsatisfying and unproductive. That was the driving force for me. I didn't know much about Teleflex before they contacted me. I certainly did my diligence but I had never worked in a medical device company before. I hadn't actually set foot in the Teleflex facility, but frankly, my decision to join was primarily based on the character and reputation of the leadership team generally, and Benson in particular. I feel I could work in most types of industry and in any stage of a company's lifecycle, public or private. Those involve skills that you can learn, but if there isn't that strong leadership connection, everything else would either fail or be very unsatisfying."

Teleflex, headquartered in Wayne, Pa., is a global provider of medical products that enhance clinical benefits, improve patient and provider safety, and reduce total procedural costs. Cam Hicks is Vice President, Global Human Resources and Employee Communication, and Benson Smith is Chairman and CEO.

Sometimes a knock on HR is that they don't get the connection to business results. The function may be a little too divorced from what actually drives the business. We were curious if

Cam's business orientation came naturally to him.

"I had certain formative experiences early on in my career that helped make me a non-traditional HR person," he told us. "I studied business in Canada. My first job when I graduated was teaching accounting at a university, so I'm very comfortable with numbers. I know a lot of HR folks are not.

"When I left teaching my first corporate job was in a life science company, where I spent my first few years in operations. I ran a P&L and had to deliver on that bottom line. The company's HR department at the time had strong technical expertise, but despite the strong core values in the company, HR as a function was not well connected to the business. So the corporate leadership intentionally reached into the business to get someone who may not have the HR technical expertise, but who understood the business and hopefully had some transferable leadership skills to make the necessary changes within the function.

"That's how I got into HR almost 25 years ago," Cam went on, "and that early operations and business background is very much a part of my wiring. When I'm talking with my HR teams, I tell them that I want us to be seen as business professionals first, HR professionals second. If we have that posture, it will keep us honest relative to the priorities that we set and will help ensure that we aren't just a functional silo in the company. Our HR professionals at Teleflex are fully embedded in the business.

"I've had the good fortune to have worked with enterprise leaders who expect business value from both me and my functions. Benson expects the same level of accountability and business performance from me as he does from any of my other executive committee colleagues."

But what if an HR team hasn't had that same business experience? How do you get them up to speed to start thinking like business partners? Cam talked about the importance of communication.

"I start every one of my HR meetings with a business update," he said. "We talk about the financials, about how the business is doing, and how HR is contributing to our overall business performance. I have a quarterly call with my whole global function, with about a hundred people on the line. We start off with the business update and go through our quarterly results. What and how you communicate helps shape your HR culture over time. It sends a message of what's most important."

That culture has gone through a transformation in the last five years. Benson Smith took over as CEO of Teleflex in 2011, having previously joined the Board of the organization in 2005. Benson hired Cam in 2013.

"When I first arrived as CEO," Benson told us, "Teleflex didn't have a clear-cut culture. There's always a culture in an organization but here it was quite different from one location to another. There was no single, unified Teleflex culture. There hadn't been much of an effort to try and establish a Teleflex brand for the employees. I certainly came into the role with some strong opinions about the importance of focusing on talent and giving people a lot of accountability and responsibility. And I was willing to acknowledge that, along with strengths, we all come with some areas of relative weakness. If we focused mainly on people's strengths and positive attributes, we would probably get more out of them than the reverse, which is too often the course that development and performance reviews take. Those reviews are more focused on the three wrong things you did in the last 22 years than on the right things you do now and how to get even better in those areas of strength. Fortunately, Cam shared a lot of that orientation."

We asked Benson and Cam to tell us what they do specifically, in terms of initiatives or projects, to coach to strengths instead of focusing on weaknesses.

"We rely on behavioral interviews to help identify good fits within the organization," Benson said. "Those interviews are a little bit different in orientation than just focusing on a person's experience or resume, and really get to the heart of their ability to build constructive, productive collaborations within and outside of the organization as well.

"Most of our employees have been through a tool we use called Talent Profiler, which helps us put a common vocabulary around their strengths. I think this approach helps generate self-awareness, a better understanding of the people that you work with, and identifies ways to improve the effectiveness of that manager/employee interface."

Benson went on to describe the limitations of traditional employee reviews.

"I was never a particular fan of annual performance reviews. There was an absolutely brilliant article in the *Harvard Business Review* several decades ago titled 'Split Roles in Performance Appraisal.' The authors looked at annual performance reviews and came to the conclusion that they were actually doing more harm than good. They can inspire a lot of resentment and defensiveness in the people being reviewed, and create disagreements about modest numerical ratings. Are you a 4.3 or a 4.2? They often focus on the few things that employees do wrong, which, in many employees' minds, is used to justify very minor differences in salary movement."

"Split Roles in Performance Appraisal" makes the following main points. Criticism has a negative effect on the achievement of goals because it creates defensiveness, and performance improves most when specific goals are established. Mutual goal setting and problem solving, not criticism, improve performance, and coaching should be a day-to-day activity, not just once-a-year. During appraisals, there should be no summary judgments or ratings.

"Without a lot of help from Cam," Benson said, "we wouldn't have initiated an alternative approach called WPRS, or Work Planning and Review System, which is also referenced in the article. It's probably taken us three years to get to the point where we're relying more and more on conversations with your manager every six weeks about the most important goals to achieve and what you think you can get done in that period of time, rather than that one-hour annual conversation where you realize you're only a 2.7 in someone's eyes."

How does Teleflex gauge the success of their non-traditional approach to assessing employees?

"There are lots of factors obviously involved in that," Cam said, "but if I look at the overall performance of the company, I'd like to think that everything we're doing from an HR perspective is adding to that business performance in some measure. We've seen a marked improvement in our retention performance. I think our talent is feeling a greater connection with their managers. We know that a lack of that connection is a big reason why folks typically leave organizations. We've also seen marked improvement in the strength of our internal talent pipeline. Of the top 30 people in the company, about 25 have either been formerly promoted or taken on a significant expansion of responsibility in the last couple of years. Those are all measures of successful progress.

"The other piece that isn't measurable, but is certainly something that I look at and our team looks at, is the quality of the performance- and talent-focused conversations within the company. They're less linked to a performance rating or to compensation. Because our WPRS approach is now woven into the organization, people are more focused on the quality of the conversations they'll be having with their managers or the goals they'll be discussing together."

Asked about what's on his plate for the future, Cam focused on continuing to develop the company's talent.

"In my opinion, talent is our single greatest rate-limiting variable looking ahead. We have a healthy balance sheet, a great catalogue of both existing and developing products, and global population and health care demographics that all point to business opportunity for many years to come. The business need for us is ensuring that we have enough of the right talent to capitalize on those opportunities. For me, talent is a crucial factor in our strategic thinking going forward.

"As we get larger and more successful as a global company, I think keeping a high bar for our HR performance is important. We need to keep asking ourselves: 'What does world class HR look like?' Raising the bar will be part of our journey forward.

"And as we get larger, how do we still preserve that entrepreneurial spirit that is both one of our core values and an important element of our culture? Our talent development strategy definitely plays a role in that."

To sum up, Cam talked about his relationship with Benson, and how it's important to wear more than one hat as an HR leader.

"Our own talents are complementary in many ways, so we're not looking for sameness there. But in terms of priorities, it's important for the HR leader to subordinate his or her views of what HR needs to do until you've got some clarity about the CEO's business priorities and the priorities of the executive team.

"You must truly be a business person first and an HR professional second. I think to earn that seat you've got to know enough of the business. You've got to be seen as credible in that regard. If you're sitting at the management table and you can't contribute to discussions about the strength of the enterprise P&L, or about plans for new products, acquisitions, or geographic expansion, then I don't think you're really going to be successful as a CHRO. You really need to have that kind of view of yourself and be prepared to deliver on those expectations.

"But there will always be a built-in tension between the two primary hats you need to wear as an HR leader," Cam went on. "Benson and the team are counting on me, more than anyone else at the executive table, to play the employee advocate role when that's required So while it's important to be a business person first, you don't want to diffuse your functional responsibility too much. As the most senior HR business partner in the company, the HR executive needs to comfortably and successfully embrace the tension that can sometimes exist between business advocacy and employee advocacy.

"You can be a more effective employee advocate if you truly understand the overall needs of the business, customers, and shareholders," Cam concluded. "Otherwise, people would rightly think, 'Cam's just advocating for what feels good for people, without understanding the business and economic realities.' If that's your personal brand before you even start the conversation, you're not going to be effective."

From Survival Mode to Growth Mode, with HR's Leadership

Tekni-Plex, Inc.
Paul J. Young, CEO
Rochelle Krombolz, Senior Vice President and
Chief Human Resources Officer

When Paul J. Young assumed leadership of Tekni-Plex, Inc. eight years ago, the company had its back to the wall.

"When I came here as a first-time CEO, the business was effectively bankrupt. It was a company that had been built up over the years by acquisitions but never integrated. We did not have one culture. We did not have one team. Nobody talked to anybody, and nobody cared about anyone else. We had businesses inside the company that actively competed against each other. A division in Europe and another one in the U.S. would price the same product differently to grab business from the other guy. There was no adult at the top really driving integration or driving culture.

"So the first step here was just to survive. We had $100 million in cash interest on our $800 million debt, with $800 million in sales and only $56 million in EBITDA. We didn't have enough cash to make the interest payments, so the company went upside down.

"My job as CEO was to start fixing it," Paul went on. "It took us probably three and a half years to do the heavy lifting, made more difficult by the backdrop of the Great Recession. We replaced every single general manager except one. We replaced almost every single plant manager. We fired most of the financial people. We closed 10 plants and let go 1,000 people. Our backs were against the wall, and we had absolutely no choice but to make these very difficult decisions. We had to survive and that was our sole focus.

"During those three years we couldn't talk about culture," Paul said. "We couldn't talk about mission, vision, or values. We talked about survival, and that was it. It took three or four years before we could look up and see a future for the company. The beauty of it was that the core of the company was solid, but somewhere along the way leadership had abdicated its responsibility and the company lost its way. The path forward wasn't complex—just difficult given the amount of work with the narrow credit agreements and debt covenants. Our people knew how much we had to do. They just wanted somebody to point the way and help them on the people side."

Thanks to the leadership of Paul and his team, including Rochelle Krombolz, Senior Vice President and Chief Human Resources Officer, Tekni-Plex is now thriving. Headquartered in Wayne, Pa., the company is a global manufacturer of technically sophisticated products and components, such as closure liners, medical tubing, high-barrier pharmaceutical films, medical compounds, dispensing components, and thermoformed containers. It operates 29 manufacturing facilities across nine countries worldwide.

"For the last three years we've been acquiring companies, investing in growth, and building our company back up," Paul told us. "We bought five businesses in the last five years. Our EBITDA was at $56 million eight years ago; today we're at $125 million. Everyone has done their part to reposition our business, get healthy, and begin to grow again.

"We're bringing in talent we probably couldn't have attracted eight years ago. Today we're attracting people from the top business schools in the US. Today, Pfizer and Novartis are customers; they weren't our customers ten years ago. Today we're setting records in our financial results. We have more growth initiatives than you can shake a stick at. We're opening a new plant in China, a new plant in Ohio, and we're integrating our acquisitions. It's almost exactly the opposite from where we were eight years ago. You can't make this kind of transformation if you don't have leadership on the HR side."

Rochelle spoke to us about her early days with the company.

"When I got here, the businesses were fairly comfortable with what they were getting from HR but I knew we could do better," she said. "We didn't have anything in terms of a talent strategy, much less function. My objective initially was to link HR to the business strategy, to propose initiatives that would have a strategic impact on the business. We could be out in front of things instead of chasing things. That means, at some level, that you have to build it before they will come.

"Some people on the HR team liked that idea," she added, "but others were rather intimidated. The first step was painting a picture of who we wanted to be in the business, and then modeling for people what that looked like, starting at the top."

For Paul, HR is not a working function if it's disconnected from business results.

"What we're trying to do with the HR function, and Rochelle has been perfect at it, is to figure out where we're driving the talent. What are the top 25 jobs that we need to put in place to hit our three-year plan? It's not easy. We've had our share of false starts and stops, but not many."

Nevertheless, as much as he believes in the power of HR to drive business results, Young was not always sold on the "softer" aspects of HR.

"When we had no mission, vision, or values, I said to Rochelle, 'Do we really need those things?' And she told me that we absolutely did need them, and that these would be tools and language for unifying the organization.

"It's only in the last few years that we've felt like one company," he said. "All of the things that I had once considered 'soft stuff' are important. Without the leadership of Rochelle and the HR department, we would have reached a plateau and not progressed any further. Rochelle wove herself into the management team. She put part of the company on her back and moved it forward."

Sometimes the leader who prevents the ship from sinking isn't the leader who brings it into port. We wondered if Paul had to change his leadership style when the company pivoted from survival mode to growth mode.

"In a survival situation, the CEO has to have control," he pointed out. "But in a situation like we're in right now, which is to grow and take some risks, you have to give up control. And that's not always an easy thing for a CEO to do.

"Today we use a group of people to interview most of our key hires. We didn't do that in the past, when I would interview candidates one-on-one; if I liked them, I hired them. A CEO can make all the decisions but you're probably not going reach optimal performance in a lot of different areas. Today we get a broader range of input in all of our business decisions.

"HR has helped me give up control through the talent they've brought into the organization," Paul told us. "If someone is better than me in a particular area, I have no ego. I'll cede control right away because I know that person fundamentally can do it better than I can. I have no claim in areas where I have no expertise. I think I'm a little different from some CEOs in that I don't need to control everything."

In echoing Paul's comments, Rochelle pointed out the loneliness of the CEO's job.

"The person in that role has great responsibility across various areas of expertise," she said. "Frankly, it's too much for one person to own all the decision-making in that position. The most effective CEOs that I've worked with are pretty self-aware. They recognize that they have areas of great strength, as well as areas that are not as strong. They actively want to surround themselves with people who are going to supplement the things that they do really well.

"That's a very vulnerable place for someone to be. Not a lot of people who operate at the top levels are willing to do that. It's unfortunate, because they set themselves up to get knocked down. Paul's an unusually humble person. I've worked with other CEOs who had to be the smartest person in the room all the time, make all the decisions, and capitalize on the airtime at every meeting. That is not an ideal leader, in my view.

"That approach shuts down the team," Rochelle went on, "in terms of collaboration, trust, creativity, and risk taking. At one point in my career I got myself sideways with a CEO, and I was advised, 'You don't have to say everything out loud, Rochelle. Maybe you should keep some things to yourself.'

"That was a really seminal moment in my career. I thought, 'You know what? This environment isn't good for me and it's not good for them. It's time to move on.' Because if I can't say what I think I need to say to be helpful, I'm not going to be as effective as I want to be, and I'm certainly not going to help the CEO get even better."

We asked Rochelle to describe the company's current HR strategy.

"Culture is first," she said. "Historically, we have managed very regionally. Now we're trying to act globally, both internally and with our customers. Previously we identified at a divisional level versus an enterprise level, which is something we're trying to change.

"We also operated in a short-term time horizon, living to fight another day, versus putting things in place that would drive rewards and returns at some future date. We've created a culture to move us from survival mode to growth mode. We've been very deliberate in articulating ideas and in creating language in the company, so that there's a shared vocabulary. We've woven that language into all of our various processes, communication systems, and reward systems, so they're constantly being reinforced and renewed.

"The second piece is talent," Rochelle continued, "and again, to Paul's point, the kinds of skills and capabilities that we needed in a distressed environment are quite different from what we need in an organization that's growing, globalizing, innovating, and taking risks. We were under-invested previously in such areas as marketing, IT, people development, M&A, and manufacturing engineering, because those weren't necessarily going to determine profitability the next day. But they are now. We've been raising the caliber of the talent in the company and evolving the structure of the organization in a way that drives collaboration, innovation, and speed.

"Paul doesn't talk about HR initiatives," she added. "He talks about business initiatives associated with people. That's really different. We changed the goals and objectives and the expectations for HR. We went back to the business and said, 'There's a higher and better use for the HR team that could have a more significant impact on the business.' It was a little risky, but when they saw that the HR people could play in the business in a different way, beyond scheduling interviews and filing the I9 forms, they liked the idea. They just hadn't seen it yet."

Rochelle spoke about the importance of an HR leader understanding where the organization is in its evolution, the problems it's trying to solve, and what the CEO is looking for in a partner.

"Insinuate yourself into business, ask business questions, learn who the customers are, and understand how your products are used. Having strong relationships with other key advisors to the CEO is really important in that regard. I work closely with the CFO, the Chief Legal Officer, and our top strategy person. Paul brings us together frequently, regardless of the topic. He doesn't talk to me only about compensation or benefits. Nor does he talk to the CFO only about financial issues. Everyone puts on their CEO hat when we're together because Paul creates that kind of environment. A lot of times CEOs will have functional, somewhat narrow conversations with individual leaders. Paul doesn't solicit input in an individual, sequential way, but rather brings us all together in one room to have a conversation.

"By doing that, we're able to have influence across functions and across the enterprise," Rochelle concluded. "We recognize the unique strengths of the other members of the team and tap into that, regardless of the topic."

In closing, we asked Paul for suggestions to other CEOs on how to best maximize the HR function in growing the business.

"First, have a process: what are you going to do first, what are you going to do second, and what are you going to do third? What are you doing this year, next year, and the year after that? Let's not surprise everybody with the 'issue du jour.' Force yourself to have a plan.

"The other point is that the hardest problems require the most talent, so I like to hire people that are pretty damn bright. You want someone smarter than you in HR. In the old manufacturing days, a lot of people defaulted into HR. That's not what you want today."

Maintaining Culture during Rapid Growth

Telerx

Linda Schellenger, President
David Desch, Chief Human Resources Officer

When a company grows substantially, it can be difficult to maintain a close and familiar culture. Such is the challenge facing Telerx, an industry-leading business process outsourcer serving Fortune 500 consumer goods and life sciences companies via a network of global contact centers. Headquartered in King of Prussia, Pa., Telerx supports clients in over 100 countries with over 30 languages, handling more than 35 million interactions per year.

"In ten years we've grown from 1,100 employees to just about 4,000 today," said Linda Schellenger, the company's President, "and from being a U.S. company to a global company with twelve locations around the world. We've grown our revenues from $65 million to $220 million.

"It's much harder to maintain the culture now that we've grown so much," she continued. "I felt like I knew almost all eleven hundred names when we were smaller. That's impossible now. When you get big, how do we maintain some of what was really good while at the same time evolve in new directions?"

Because the company is an outsourcer, Telerx is not just one big company where everyone is doing the same thing. For example, there's a Pfizer team, a Merck team, a Nestle team, and a Campbell's team.

"Those teams make people feel like they're part of a small company," Linda told us. "They become very tight and very close. This has allowed us to keep a little bit of a smaller company feel in what is now a much larger company.

"As we develop our strategic plan for 2017 and beyond, how do we continue to make people feel that way? It can be hard to feel valued in a large organization. There aren't many companies that can do that really well. That's the challenge that we must take on and conquer."

Closely involved in facing that challenge is David Desch, Chief Human Resources Officer, who has more than 20 years of experience managing both global and domestic HR organizations.

"We're at an inflection point, given that we've added global locations through an acquisition about two years ago," Dave said. "We're starting to put in more controls in the global part of the organization. We have to make sure that we're focusing just as much on the culture of those places. The further away from the center, the more you need to make sure that you're doing things the right way.

"And as you become global," he added, "you have to be really sensitive to the cultures within those countries. Europeans feel very differently about their personal and vacation time. It's not easy to have programs and policies that drive revenue and margin, and that at the same time honor the cultural piece. However, we must find that balance."

Linda brings an HR perspective to her leadership at Telerx, having worked as HR leader at TCIM Services in the early 2000s.

"We ran customer service contact centers and had about 5,000 people around the world. It was a busy, busy place, and I learned a lot. I loved being an HR person. I couldn't imagine doing anything else until I had the opportunity to enter general management."

We asked Linda how that foundation comes into play in making decisions and guiding Telerx.

"I really understand and appreciate the value of the people in our company, and the need to keep them motivated. But in some ways having an HR background can make my job tougher. It's fun to be a leader when everything's going great and you're hiring people. It's not so much fun when you need to do a reduction in force. Am I slower to the punch at those times? Or am I tougher about it because I've been in an HR position and, based on the facts, I know what we need to do? I feel I'm more sensitive to the people issues and am much more willing to listen to those issues than CEOs who have had no HR training."

Dave mentioned supervisor and manager development as a major HR initiative Telerx wants to undertake.

"We do a really good job of on-boarding people into the call center and teaching them the technical skills, but we could offer them more support after that. We're working to improve supervisory management development. About 75% of our frontline supervisors come from hourly staff. A lot of regional leaders who are directing them come from hourly staff. If you want high engagement, those supervisors are the ones who are going to determine that engagement. We need to train them— whether it's online, in person, through coaching or shadowing—so that they can develop the necessary skills to be effective as supervisors. We're trying to do this in a way that works in a global call center environment."

We asked Linda how Telerx measures employee engagement.

"We've done employee satisfaction surveys every twenty-four months within each of our sites. Our scores have always been in the eighties, mid-eighties, which is very high in customer service. Still, we're trying to morph ourselves more into the engagement model versus the employee satisfaction model."

"It's very difficult when you have, on average, a 35% turnover rate in the business," added Dave, "and sometimes much, much higher. As a BPO provider, we need to provide our services at a lower cost than our customers can, which puts pressure on wages, the biggest cost component of our service. Given these conditions, we've done a good job of doing the things needed to help drive satisfaction."

Linda pointed out that minimum wage changes could affect their business drastically. "How do we make that work? Even the laws for overtime are changing. The regulatory landscape over the next 24 to 36 months is going to have a great impact on our company. Not necessarily bad, but we just have to figure out how we work within the new regulatory environment."

We asked Dave for the advice he would give to an HR leader to forge the kind of close working relationship he has with Linda.

"First, learn the business. It is absolutely critical that you're not seen as someone who's just focused on HR programs. It's about making sure that HR goals are well aligned with the business goals. Understand the business and then figure out what decision making opportunities will influence the organization in a way that the CEO will respond to most effectively. What could have the quickest impact on the business?

"The ability to build trust is absolutely critical. If that trust doesn't exist, then you won't get invited to be involved in all aspects of the business. You won't have influence on the leader or the rest of the leadership team.

"Linda's a much better listener than many CEOs I've worked with," Dave continued. "The organization that I came from, while my input was listened to and sought, the trust never quite developed. It was the style of the CEO to make most decisions without necessarily either getting consensus or seeing value in other points of view."

Linda added: "A confidant and trusted advisor relationship is one of the keys to success. I can say what I'm thinking without fear of it being taken out of context or in the wrong way. We can talk about issues in a real way. You need a partner to whom you can say, 'Thanks for letting me vent and for helping me solve the problem.' If you don't have that kind of honest relationship, it's a tough way to go. We help each other be objective about things, to get to the right business and people decisions."

Dave pointed out that he can maintain neutrality by not having allegiance to any particular person on the team, but not to the point where he doesn't have a point of view or perspective.

"I do have a perspective," he said. "It's important that I represent my perspective, but I also can represent other perspectives when she needs to hear it. I sit in the office right next to Linda and the CFO is two offices down. Linda said, 'I expect the CFO and HR to be Switzerland. You guys aren't part of the business unit. Therefore, you need to be looking at it objectively and tell me when we're getting off track, or if you're hearing from others that we're getting off track.'"

"For me," Linda added, "the CFO and the HR leader are the two most critical people when it comes to objectivity. Yes, operations and sales are crucial, but they're presenting you with very measurable and finite kinds of information. Some of the most crucial information is soft information. You might say, 'Well, the CFO, that's not very soft. It's all numbers.' That's true, but you need to dig through how people are representing the numbers to get to the reality. We can all make the numbers say whatever we'd like them to say. The HR person, along with everybody on the team, has to have a pretty objective view.

"It's important that Dave can step out of being a peer to the people he works with and become the HR person to me. When I say I'm concerned about so and so, or that so and so is not engaged, or when I ask whether he's seeing what I'm seeing, Dave can step away from being their peer and, for better or worse, be objective. That's not easy to do."

Traditionally, or maybe even stereotypically, a lot of HR leaders may say that they don't get along with finance, and vice versa. But that doesn't seem to be a problem at Telerx.

"I have seen it with other CFO's, who believe that HR should report under them," Linda said. "That's not a good thing to say to me. I believe HR should sit at the table, especially when you're in the service business. I'm not sure how you do it without that voice.

"Our CFO is tough when it comes to expenses, but I think Dave is very balanced about making the right business decisions. They have mutual respect in listening to each other's opinions. I'm not fighting that fight here, but it happens often in other companies. The HR person needs a seat at the table just like the CFO or COO. If you give that person a lesser role, you'll get lesser results."

Aligning with the Business to Drive Success

Virtua

Richard P. Miller, President and CEO
Rhonda Jordan, Senior Vice President and
Chief Human Resources Officer

"I've been a CEO now for 21 years," said Richard P. Miller, President and CEO of Virtua, the non-profit healthcare system that is south Jersey's largest healthcare provider. "When I started as a CEO, I had a different thought process about HR. Back in the '80s and '90s, it was more about personnel than it was about human resources.

"I think a lot of people's mindsets around HR have evolved. If you look at some of the bigger companies, such as GE, HR is held in very high esteem. I've talked to Jeff Immelt about this, because GE is a great people organization. We've taken a lot of their ideas, adapted them, and made them our own."

Headquartered in Mount Holly, N.J., Virtua operates a network of hospitals, surgery centers, physician practices, and fitness centers.

"We've become very good at transforming things," Miller continued. "Back in 2001, 2002, we were an average organization. We were at the 50th percentile in everything. We instituted a people review process that allowed us to find out who's accountable and who's not accountable in the organization. We reviewed all of their goals and objectives with measurable results, to find out if we had the right players. Now there is

70

nowhere for management to hide. If you look at Virtua's success over the past ten, fifteen years, it's about the people and talent in the organization. That's why the HR and CEO partnership is so important.

"I don't spend any of my time on the personnel functions of HR," Rich pointed out. "I spend my time on the growth areas in HR—organizational effectiveness, leadership development, and talent development. To me, those are the areas that are critical. Every HR leader should report to the CEO. If you're not driving success with people, then you're not going to be successful. It's as simple as that."

Rhonda Jordan is Virtua's Senior Vice President and Chief Human Resources Officer.

"When I started out at Virtua," she said, "I wanted the organization to know that we understood the business and that what we do is aligned with the business. Once we developed that strategy, I met with all my EVPs and shared the strategy. What would they add? What would they change? What did we want to do in order to continuously develop?

"In my first meeting with Rich, I told him, 'While I definitely know that we have a great relationship, the CEO role is the loneliest role in the organization. I hope that as we continue to work together, that I can be a trusted confidante for you."

At the same time, Rhonda said she pushes back when needed.

"Oh, easily," said Miller. "Rhonda will tell me if she doesn't think if it's a good idea to do something, or if she feels we're not going in the right direction. That's what I'm looking for.

I want her to say to me, 'Hey Rich, I don't think you're headed in the right direction with this, or this is not a good way to go.'"

Throughout our interview, Miller emphasized HR's strategic importance. "Rhonda provides me with a different perspective about strategy. I tell Rhonda that she's not in this room as an HR person, but as a valued strategic partner."

We asked Rhonda to go into more detail about the HR strategy that has been so important to Virtua's success.

"Our vision is to be the best integrated talent management function, where people come to us for best practices. We align our strategies based on achieving that, but also on connecting to the business. Second, we have a focus on leadership development. We have a focus on talent and insuring that we're bringing in the right talent. We have the assessments that are able to support that.

"Third is technology," Rhonda added, "because we want to be able to provide the organization with the best tools and data. Right now it's cumbersome to get information out of our current system. We're very paper intensive, as we're still doing paper evaluations. Our focus is on looking at something new in the performance management process. One of the things we're toying with is doing reviews quarterly instead of annually, and technology is going to help us with that. We want to make sure we don't put in a system that becomes more cumbersome for employees, but we definitely want something that's easier and gives our employees the feedback they need."

Miller told us more about Virtua's talent review process.

"We spend two days, twice a year, reviewing people who we think are going to grow the organization in the future. The senior leaders sit down together and identify people who may be ready to move to a new position. We look at their talent level and talk about how we can help that person grow. A great example is an employee who started in HR and now is running all of our hospitals at Virtua.

"We'll take a group of people we're reviewing out to lunch," Rich told us. "We'll ask them: what are you thinking about in the next five or six years for yourself? What do you want to do? Senior leadership has that discussion with middle management, to find out what they're thinking.

We may assume we know what's good for them but they need to tell us what's good for them.

The other thing we try to do is to grow our people through education. We have various leadership courses at Virtua. We start preparing people to move up the chain of leadership, so they understand what it takes to be an executive vice president or another senior leader. I work with Rhonda to develop that process, to get people well positioned for the future. The talent development process is probably the most important thing senior leadership does here."

We asked Rhonda to share some instances where she influenced Rich's thinking from an HR point of view and how that has impacted the organization.

"We redesigned out leadership development strategy and Rich has been aligned with that. I was concerned we might be getting survey fatigue. I suggested we get feedback from our employees every other year. Rich was hesitant about that. He said, 'Well, Rhonda, how am I going to know what our employees are thinking?'

"That's where our employee change teams, which Rich established throughout the company, step in. They focus on employee engagement and customer satisfaction. I said, 'We're going to get the feedback that way, and then you have representatives from those teams on our employee advisory group.' He loved the idea."

Virtua has thirteen employee change teams throughout the company. Representatives from each of those teams attend the employee advisory group, composed of thirty employees that Miller meets with on a bimonthly bias.

"It's not a complaint session," Rich told us. "It's not about the coffee not being hot in my area. It's very positive. We talk about issues that affect patient care, that affect their lives, employee engagement and recognition, things of that nature. It's a problem-solving group.

"I basically say to the employees, if there's a problem, go figure it out. I want them to own it. I say to them, 'You think I know everything. You're going to find out how little I do know.' The group just relaxes and we have a lot of great conversations. The employee advisory group gets them engaged, and they go back and get their employees engaged—here's what we learned and here's what we need to do to improve things, whether it's patient care or customer service. I'm not a rules based guy. If employees can do something to improve things, we'll step out of our box a little bit and ask them to show us how to do it. It's been a great process.

"We have another process called shared governance. For example, nurses and other patient care staff will come together and talk about how they can improve patient care. I try to attend a handful of those.

"I was listening in on a meeting of the neonatal intensive care nurses (NICU)," Rich told us. "They were saying how difficult it is for the nurses to warm milk for neonates when there are up to fifty babies in the unit. The temperature of the milk has to be perfect for these babies, because they're so small. They said that there's equipment that can warm the milk. I said, 'How much is the equipment?' It turns out the cost is $1,000 per warmer and they needed forty of them. We purchased the warmers within a two-week period.

"We have to be an open organization that accepts that kind of information and acts on it. But we first have to empower our people to give us that information."

Rich talked about the example he wants to set for how the rest of the organization behaves and pointed out that he conducts Virtua's new employee orientation every week, which is unheard of for a CEO.

"I'm able to connect to new employees directly. The feedback I've gotten from them has been off the charts. A lot of them say they've never seen a CEO at orientation, particularly a company with 9,000 employees. Not that many CEOs are going to take the time to do that. I think it's important to show your people how much you care about them and how important they are to building the organization.

"I love engaging with people. I have so much fun with employees. Take the opportunities to re-engage. Don't be sitting in an office shuffling papers and signing things. Get out and be visible to your employees. It's not as easy for us anymore, with over 9,000 people here. It's hard to get to everything, but engage with people as much as you can."

Transforming a Company's Mindset

Ricoh Americas
Martin Brodigan, Chairman and CEO
Donna Venable, Executive Vice President, Human Resources

Changing a company's culture can be a daunting task for any organization, but it's particularly challenging after a merger or acquisition, when two entirely different cultures have to learn to work together. Such was the challenge facing the management of Ricoh Americas after the company's 2008 acquisition of Ikon Office Solutions.

Headquartered in Malvern, Pa., Ricoh Americas is the North and South American arm of Tokyo-based Ricoh Company, Ltd., the Japanese multinational imaging and electronics company. It employs 30,000 people throughout North and South America. In the late 1990s through early 2000s, Ricoh grew to become the largest copier manufacturer in the world, acquiring, in addition to Ikon, Savin Corp., Gestetner, Lanier Worldwide Inc., Rex Rotary, Monroe Nashuatec, and most recently IBM Printing Systems Division/Infoprint Solutions Company.

"When I took over the role as CEO in 2012," Martin Brodigan told us, "we had to finish the integration of the two companies into one culture. And then we had to fundamentally change the company to a new business model. That's all about changing people's mindsets, changing people's behaviors, and in some cases building new talent. So our top priorities all involved people. HR is people, so that to me is the clear link through all this change."

As we learned again and again in our interviews, CEOs tend to fall into two categories. One category believes that HR plays a defensive role focused on compliance, regulation, and administration. The other group believes that HR can really help drive organizational transformation and performance. Martin unequivocally belongs to the second group.

"The key to me has always been to get the most out of your people and the numbers will follow. Philosophically, I just believe that's the right way to go, to get everyone wanting to go in the same direction. It's a lot easier to have them pushing you along rather than you dragging them along.

"There were job restructuring changes that had to happen," Martin continued. "First of all, we were very top heavy on management from the two companies. We had overlap, perhaps even competition, internal competition, which is even more destructive. About 30% of our VPs and above either took a position below VP or left the company.

"Since we acquired Ikon in 2008, we had been operating in this quasi-merged fashion. We were one company, but we weren't operating as one company. In fact, five or six years ago, everyone would introduce themselves by saying 'I'm from Ikon,' or 'I'm from Lanier,' or 'I'm from Savin.' There was a lot of urban legend about what you could do and couldn't do, and what your role was and wasn't. But we needed to move forward as one company, and to do so meant changing the mindset of the organization. Today we have a lot cleaner line of sight, cleaner titles. Just a lot more clarity about where people fit in and what the mission is. And HR played a critical role in this transformation."

Donna Venable, Executive Vice President, Human Resources at Ricoh Americas, filled us in on the major initiatives HR pursued to drive the cultural and organizational transformation.

"A key step was the process of defining people's roles," she said. "That may sound very basic but it's often not, especially when you're integrating so many companies. What were people expected to do within the organization? What responsibilities or decision making did they have?

Did we need more folks who understood systems integration or technical architecture for a customer? Who understood networks? How would we deploy our solutions and equipment to best meet the customer's needs?"

We were curious about the people aspects of that transformation, especially in the core business, where employees may not feel as important to the organization following a major acquisition.

"That's exactly how people can feel," Donna agreed. "Change management is always extremely difficult. You want people to understand how they fit within the organization, where the organization is going, and the value they can bring to the company. We need to define that for them and that starts at the top. You have to publicly and openly talk about the value in the organization that has brought us to where we are today, and the value that will come into play as our customers' needs evolve. It's really helping people understand that they can change and evolve as the organization is changing and evolving, and that if they do so the opportunities are great for everyone.

"And HR has facilitated this transformation," Donna told us. "We spend a lot of time focusing on communication and culture building skills. It started with a conversation I had with Martin about how to get people to really talk and listen to each other, instead of talking at each other or giving lip service, which is common in many companies. How do we break down the silos? What can we do differently?

"Our HR team thought about ways to accomplish that. We didn't want it over-engineered. It needed to be simple, very straightforward, and something that was learned from the top. So we built the Leadership Connection Initiative. It started with Martin and his direct reports speaking to the next 125 leaders in the organization. Each month was devoted to a specific topic. What were the clear definitions we would use throughout the company so that we were all on the same page? How were we going to interact and behave? What was our definition of collaboration? How do we have the tough conversations when someone isn't delivering to the team?

"Those 125 leaders would then have the same conversation with the next 600 people in the organization. And those 600 would have discussions with their teams. In any given month, the same topics are being discussed across the entire organization, bringing clarity to how we communicate and collaborate.

"The result was that we opened dialogue across functional, geographic, business unit, and organizational lines so that employees were speaking with people they wouldn't normally interact with. They were hearing new perspectives that were very different from their team's perspectives. After acquisitions, people tend to stay within the same network they had in the company that was acquired. They stick with what's familiar—their own language and reference points. The Leadership Connection Initiative helped break down barriers, forge relationships, and really unpack the organization. So regardless of what company you originally worked for, this is the new Ricoh way."

Martin and Donna are clear that HR leaders and their teams need to be business people first.

"Donna has a great ability to engage with our various leaders on the business problems they're trying to solve," Martin told us. "Too often HR departments will carry out the will of the business leader. Instead, Donna will say, 'What's the underlying challenge? We need to understand the root causes of the problem, then align with the action that drives the best result in the business.'"

"You have to understand the business," Donna agreed. "In HR there's still too often the view that that's not necessary. But you have to know what tools are most appropriate to meet business needs. HR is your function, but you've got to be immersed in the business and understand what you're doing and how it can impact results. I think that's why engaging directly with customers is so important to our HR team. When they understand our customers and have firsthand knowledge of their needs, they can have a different discussion with our business unit leaders and their teams about what they see as our strengths and our weaknesses, and what kind of talent to bring to Ricoh."

A challenge in many organizations is creating an environment where people feel that contrary opinions will be welcomed and not punished. We asked Donna about that issue at Ricoh Americas.

"It's a process of freeing up people's ability to speak up," she said. "If they can't speak up, they shut down. I don't know if you can get 100% there until people have experienced speaking up. Once they do, they become extremely open about it. That's when you start to have the kind of engagement that allows you to get to core issues that might have been overlooked.

"I remember a discussion between a sales leader and the leader of the supply chain that hadn't taken place in the past. Changes made by the supply chain organization had created a very specific and narrow product situation for the sales team, yet they hadn't had that conversation. Because we created an opportunity to talk about both the positives and the negatives, it changed the way they interacted.

"By challenging employees in a different way," Donna continued, "by being honest, transparent, and communicative with them, we're showing them how they can participate. The fact that we're defining communication and collaboration creates expectations in employees. HR takes a lead in the messaging and communication part of the process. We do a lot of pulse surveys. We survey 25% of our employees every three months. The surveys help us identify where in the organization we have challenges. We recently did a survey to understand more about collaboration because we didn't feel we were making as much progress there. We were making dramatic progress across the board, but this was one place where we really wanted to see stronger movement, so we used a follow-up survey for greater insight.

"There have been dramatic challenges through all of our transformation," she said, summing up. "As leaders, we must have the ability to listen, to get the pulse of the organization and understand what's going on. To take action where we need to, to push where we need to, and to back off where we need to. It works because we have a high level of collaboration and interaction. The direction we're going is to fundamentally change the organization."

Never Under-Invest in Human Resources

Johnson Controls
George R. Oliver, President and COO
Larry Costello, Executive Vice President and
Chief Human Resources Officer

"Human Resources is probably the single most important position in any company, not only in contributing to strategy development, but in deploying human capital to execute that strategy," George Oliver told us. "Since I became a CEO, I've learned so much more about the science of HR than I knew previously. There's so much more to the function than just hiring and firing. The science is much more strategic."

George R. Oliver is President and Chief Operating Officer of Johnson Controls, a global leader in building products and technology, integrated solutions, and energy storage. The company was created on Sept. 2, 2016, by the merger of Tyco International PLC, the world's largest fire protection and security company, with Johnson Controls Inc., the global leader in building controls and HVAC systems. Oliver had previously been CEO of Tyco, which had 57,000 employees in 50 countries and $10 billion in annual revenue. He now has responsibility for leading the integration of the two companies, and is relying on a robust HR strategy to make that happen.

"I probably spend more time with our HR leader than I spend with anyone," Oliver told us. "With human capital, you get feedback every day. There are lots of challenges and change is constant—organizational change, people change, and then managing through that change

80

successfully to make sure the business is supported. It's not change for the sake of change, but change that's needed to be to be successful.

"And the speed of all of that is accelerating. What worked 10 or 20 years ago from a human capital standpoint doesn't work today. It's not only about having the skill sets, but having maturity across the organization to deploy those skill sets. The HR person needs to have the maturity to be a partner with the CEO, as well as a team member who can enable the success of individual team members."

As CEO of Tyco, Oliver led its transformation from a holding company to an operating company, with a sharp focus on leveraging technology and innovation to advance its leadership position in the industry.

"When we launched 'the new Tyco' back in September of 2012," he said, "we recognized that our human capital was the most important element in being able to execute our strategy. Our previous model was that of a holding company, with businesses operating somewhat independently, running their own HR functions and the like. I had the opportunity to bring in a new HR leader, Larry Costello, who had significant experience in building world-class HR teams across multiple industries. With Larry's experience and leadership, we built some real depth into each of the key HR functions that could be leveraged across the organization, as opposed to every business unit and region doing their own thing. That's the journey we've been on. We've transformed lots of systems, structures, and capabilities to support a world-class HR function."

We asked Oliver to go into more detail about the different processes and systems that have been implemented to foster real change in the organization.

"Right out of the gate, we launched what we call our Leadership Essentials. How do we define leadership? What's essential to being successful within the new company? What are the skill sets that need to be developed?

"Then we began to assess our leaders on those essentials. That was foundational to the development plans that were ultimately put into place. All of that was talent acquisition and development. We streamlined all of our job classifications into one structure, so that we not only have the ability to be market competitive with how we compensate, but to make sure that we're competitive in attracting the talent.

"Then on the other side, the sales comp went from hundreds of plans to something more streamlined, to making sure that we're extremely strategic in how we build the plans. It's oriented more towards quota systems and building in productivity, and then enabling that with the tools and systems required to ultimately be successful. Talent acquisition, talent development, the job structure compensation—those are the big elements, the big pieces, that we put into place."

Now that Johnson Controls and Tyco are merging, we wondered about HR's role in that transition and Oliver's assessment of its effectiveness.

"The most important work we do in any type of merger situation," Oliver told us, "is around people and culture. We need to make sure that all of our talent has an opportunity to play within the new structure and get the right type of opportunities. Then defining what we want the future state to be, and then translating that into mission, values, behaviors, and practices that ultimately position the combined company to be successful.

"The single biggest cultural change that we committed to from day one back in 2012 was to do 'zero harm.' We're a life safety company. We've reduced our exposure from an accident standpoint. Our injuries are down over 50%. And the impact that we've had on the environment is down about 15%."

Oliver told us that his views of HR were formed when he went to work for GE right out of college, at their operation in Lynn, Mass., where the HR leader was Bill Conaty. Conaty, who served 15 years as Senior Vice President of Human Resources at GE and later managed the CEO transition process from Jack Welch to Jeff Immelt, helped shape the modern face of HR.

"Conaty had a very big influence on me," Oliver told us. "And we all learned from Jack Welch, who put a priority on human capital and human resources. We all learned that the most important work you do, as you move up an organization as a leader, is accessing, promoting, and developing future leaders, and building the domain and capabilities that are critical to a particular business model. Those were the fundamentals that I built into HR and human capital, to create a world-class function that would move Tyco forward."

We asked George to go into more detail about his relationship with Larry Costello, who served as Executive Vice President and CHRO at Tyco.

"In my view, the three critical roles supporting a CEO are HR, finance, and general counsel. Larry has contemporized the function so that HR is very proactive. Many times he can be the most strategic person in the room, whether we're talking about strategy, business models, compensation structures, or organizational structures. He has great insight into how markets work and how different business models are supported with human capital, not only in types of talent, but in the mix of talent required to be successful. In today's environment companies need speed in order to win, given the rapid changes in business models and technology. That requires HR being involved on the front end in configuring strategy, and the changes needed to attract and utilize talent.

"When you go through a transformation like we went through," Oliver went on, "people's views of HR change. They realize the value of HR in accelerating their success as leaders and the company's success. It's fascinating to see."

We asked Costello to give us his views on how he works with Oliver, not only in transforming Tyco but in managing the recent merger.

"My role was to help George, as a new CEO, through our transformative process," Costello said. "We can't predict where that transformation will take us. I recognize that creating an operating company that is the world's largest foreign security company is significant but at the end of the day, on a standalone basis, these companies have different defining moments. The question is whether you can continue to sustain 13%-15% EPS growth each year without a more aggressive M&A strategy.

"George and I have hours of conversation about what he believes in as a CEO. What are the most important attributes or characteristics that you want to create in the business? What is your vision? What goals do you want to achieve and what are the messages that you want to resonate throughout the organization? Are we going to be a performance-based culture? Are we going to be a company that leans on technology? Do we want to be a growth company? What are the things that resonate? Those questions have implications from an HR perspective.

"At the companies where I worked earlier in my career, these conversations didn't take place. Back then, HR was strictly a functional organization and business leaders would generally ignore it. In the 80s and 90s, HR experienced serious cost-cutting and rightsizing. During that time, I recognized that you couldn't survive in HR from a cost-cutting perspective unless you created a business equation that worked."

As a result of that early experience, Costello realized that HR leaders needed to have the courage to be change agents within their companies.

"But you can never be a change agent," he said, "without being prepared. Being prepared isn't just another program and a process; it's having the business acumen to understand what value you're trying to create and the impact it's going to have. It means doing your homework, understanding the business, and understanding what the CEO wants.

"We're investing somewhere around four and a half billion dollars in people, in a company that's ten billion in size. Almost half the spend. That's not insignificant. Now, what are all the components that make up that spend? I'm able to talk to George from a business standpoint. I start with the equation of how the business actually operates. I've done my homework, which requires acumen, analytics, and data. Now I can speak George's language. I understand the economics of how we go to business in each of our product categories.

"I think we all know that successful CEOs don't try to do everything," Larry continued. "They pick four or five things that resonate with the external community, with the employees.

"Once you understand the value system, then you begin to translate it into how you optimize and unleash human capital to achieve your objectives. When I get a pretty good strategic feel, the CEO and I become totally aligned. We know what to expect from an investment standpoint, and then we begin to create the structure through a robust and very talented team. When I can get that right, HR changes from being viewed as just an expense center to being a valued contributor."

Our conversation then turned to productivity and HR's role in driving it.

"The test for me is visiting a plant or going into the sales world," Costello told us, "and asking people if they personally see the intended value of what we're doing. Are they getting productivity from that particular process or program? If the answer is yes, I can go to George and say I have increased the level of satisfaction by the investment we made. You don't have to be a brain surgeon to realize that satisfaction gives you productivity. That's how the entire culture begins to evolve and continues to develop. I can go into an annual operating plan review or a quarterly review with confidence.

"It sounds simple but it's very hard," Larry went on. "If George says we need 5% productivity year-over-year, I say here's the deal—I'll give you 5%, but you need to give me half of that back for reinvestment so I can continue to nurture the investment we're all looking for. That investment might be expanding the curriculum for leadership development or be used to make us more strategic around talent acquisition. It could be a variety of different things. At the end of the day, I know he's going to give me half of it back because I've always delivered for him.

"So, as a result, I've taken HR and made it a business. All of the leaders on my team, whether it's the person who heads talent or technology, all of them have a budget. They're treated like a businessperson, so they act like GMs. They know they're going to be held accountable for that spend and productivity requirement. They are measured just the way George measures me. At the end of each year, they need to come to me with priorities that are aligned with the business leaders. Because George sees the tangible benefit that comes from this approach, he knows we can't stop investing in HR."

In concluding our interview, Oliver stressed the importance of that investment: "Never under-hire in HR, because the magnitude of its impact on an organization is huge. From a compensation standpoint, certainly you want to be competitive in your market, but I've learned never to under-hire in HR. Instead, I would over-hire, because HR has enormous value in building the right capabilities across an entire organization."

Afterword

You've heard a lot of great advice and gained many insights from the CEOs and HR leaders we interviewed. There's a lot to reflect on, and to help with that reflection we'd like to summarize what we feel are the main points made in this book. We hope you can apply these insights and values to your own business, in building a powerful working relationship to drive results.

--To form a powerful team, the CEO and HR leader need to have a close and trusting relationship, based on candor and honesty and the ability to give frank feedback when needed.

--The HR leader needs to be pro-active in establishing that relationship, not by adhering to HR's traditional roles, but by searching out ways to add value to the organization, by complementing the CEO's talents and abilities, and by looking for ways to make a major impact on the company's performance.

--The HR leader should have a role in the organization equal to the COO, CFO, and other leaders on the business side of operations. The HR leader is as responsible and accountable for driving business results as these leaders, and the CEO and senior executives need to view the HR leader as an equal on the leadership team.

--The HR leader's and team's understanding of the business has to be equal to or greater than their understanding of HR issues.

--A deep understanding of the business allows the HR leader to recruit and develop talent that can lead to transformational change.

--An HR leader needs to be strategic and not reactive or tactical. The strategy and tactics of the HR team need to match the overall strategy and tactics of the business.

--By taking a lead role in improving communication in the organization and breaking down "silos," the HR team can be instrumental in changing a company's culture.

--Positive cultural changes can drive a company's performance and those changes cannot take place without the strategic orientation of the HR team. A large part of this is teaching employees throughout every level of the organization about their strategic role in the company—what they need to know and do in order to drive performance.

--An HR leader can help establish a common language throughout an organization, so that employees are working from a shared value system toward shared goals.

--A major role played by HR is finding out what employees truly think about the company and acting on that information to improve culture. A positive and engaged culture plays a critical role in driving results.

--HR is responsible not just for hiring the right talent but assimilating it into the organization and using it to the fullest to achieve strategic ends. HR should be in the forefront of creating the organizational designs or structures to address obstacles that stand in the way of talent management.

--The HR leader gains credibility as an employee advocate by being a businessperson first and an HR leader second. The most effective employee advocate is someone who truly understands the business.

We hope this book will help you open a dialogue in your business about the role of HR across functional, geographic, business unit, and organizational lines. We hope the shared experience of the executives in this book will help your employees and management work together in more creative and effective ways, by opening new lines of communication and sharing new perspectives. By forming a powerful team, CEOs and HR leaders can help break down barriers, forge productive relationships, and lead their companies to new heights.

Company Profiles

Citadel Federal Credit Union is a financial institution offering a full-range of banking products and services with deposits federally insured up to $250,000. Established in 1937 as the credit union for Lukens Steel Company, today Citadel has more than 190,000 customers and over $2.8 billion in assets. Many things have changed throughout our 80-year history, but our commitment to serving our customers, and the communities in which they live and work, has not.

Houghton International Inc. is a global leader in delivering advanced metalworking fluids and services for the automotive, aerospace, metals, mining, machinery, offshore, and beverage industries. With headquarters in Valley Forge, Pa., Houghton operates research, manufacturing, and office locations in 33 countries around the world, delivering fluid solutions that increase profitability, improve product quality, and minimize risks for our customers.

HPE Financial Services serves as the bridge between technology and finance solutions to help customers meet their IT goals. With flexible payment options and IT Asset Management capabilities that support the entire IT lifecycle, HPE Financial Services can partner with customers to build investment strategies that work best for their businesses.

Lassonde Pappas and Co. is a North American leader in private label beverage manufacturing committed to customer and consumer satisfaction. We are the #1 organic private label beverage and cranberry sauce producer in the U.S. *From concept to shelf,* Lassonde Pappas strives to provide the best in-class experience with category insights and innovative solutions. Lassonde Pappas remains committed to our small town roots and rural values. Hardworking and caring are qualities that make Lassonde Pappas special. Since 1942, we've been producing delicious products for our customers.

With over 100 years of experience, **PMA Companies** ranks among the nation's top providers of workers' compensation and other property and casualty insurance products, as well as third-party administration services. At PMA, we leverage the depth and breadth of our expertise to help clients take a smarter, more strategic approach to managing risk and reducing its total cost. PMA clients also benefit from our service-driven culture and our commitment to delivering tangible value to the organizations we serve.

NFI Industries is a fully integrated third-party supply chain solutions provider. Serving customers around the world and across a variety of industries, NFI is dedicated to providing customized, engineered solutions that propel a business to succeed. NFI's business lines include dedicated transportation, warehousing, intermodal, brokerage, transportation management, global, and real estate services.

Privately held by the Brown family since its inception in 1932, NFI generates more than $1.2 billion in annual revenue and employs more than 8,000 associates. NFI operates 29 million square feet of warehouse and distribution space, and its company-owned fleet consists of over 2,200 tractors and 8,200 trailers.

Publicis Health is the world's premier healthcare communications, media, medical education, and sales network. With 15 brands in more than 40 offices across the globe, Publicis Health helps clients harness the velocity of change through the alchemy of creativity and technology. Publicis Health brands include: Digitas Health LifeBrands, Discovery USA, Heartbeat Ideas, in-sync, Langland, Maxcess Managed Markets,

PDI, Publicis Health Media, Publicis LifeBrands Medicus, Publicis Touchpoint Solutions, Razorfish Health, Saatchi & Saatchi Wellness, Tardis Medical Consulting, and Verilogue. Publicis Health has been named by *Advertising Age* as the largest healthcare communications network by revenue for the past six years. Publicis Health is a division of Publicis Groupe S.A.

Rentokil Initial is one of the largest business services companies in the world, operating in Europe, North America, South America, Asia Pacific, and Africa. The company has over 66,000 employees and provides a range of support services to over 1.5 million customers in 60 countries around the world. The organization operates multiple brands that deliver residential and commercial pest control services, as well as offering hygiene, interior landscaping, and food safety and operational assessment services to business customers.

Rentokil began operations in North America in the early 1980s. Since then, the company has grown its operations to cover the entire United States, Canada, and Mexico. In 2016, Rentokil's Pest Management business in the U.S. and Canada began operations under the national umbrella of Rentokil Steritech, reflecting Rentokil North America's acquisition of The Steritech Group, Inc., the premier provider of commercial pest management services in North America.

Customers of Rentokil Steritech in the United States are serviced by its three highly regarded regional brands: Ehrlich in the Eastern U.S., Presto-X in the Central U.S., and Western Exterminator in the Western U.S. In Canada, operations provide service under the Rentokil Steritech name, and in Mexico, under Rentokil.

Rentokil North America also operates two other business service companies in the U.S., providing a complete line of care for its customers. Ambius specializes in interior landscaping and premium scenting to enhance environments, while our Steritech Brand Standards business provides food safety and operational excellence assessments to help companies mitigate risk and drive growth.

Ricoh is a global technology company that has been transforming the way people work for more than 80 years. Under its corporate tagline—"imagine. change."—Ricoh continues to empower companies and individuals with services and technologies that inspire innovation, enhance sustainability and boost business growth. These include document management systems, IT services, production print solutions, visual communications systems, digital cameras, and industrial systems. Headquartered in Tokyo, Ricoh Group operates in approximately 200 countries and regions. For further information, please visit www. ricoh.com.

Solenis International LP manufactures specialty chemicals for process, water treatment, functional chemistries, and monitoring and control systems. It serves customers in a wide range of industries: bio refining, chemical processing, industrial water, mining and mineral processing, municipal, oil and gas, packaging paper and board, power generation, printing and writing papers, pulp, tissue and towel, and specialties and wood adhesives.

Tekni-Plex Inc. is a globally-integrated company focused on developing and manufacturing innovative packaging materials, medical compounds, and precision-crafted tubing solutions for some of the most well-known names in the medical, pharmaceutical, personal care, household and industrial, and food and beverage markets. Headquartered in Wayne, Pa., Tekni-Plex employs 2,500 people throughout its operations in Belgium, China, Costa Rica, Germany, India, Italy, Northern Ireland, and the U.S.

Teleflex, headquartered in Wayne, Pa., is a global provider of medical technologies designed to improve the health and quality of people's lives. The company applies purpose driven innovation—a relentless pursuit of identifying unmet clinical needs—to benefit patients and healthcare providers around the world. The company's product portfolio encompasses the fields of vascular and interventional access, surgical, anesthesia, cardiac care, urology, emergency medicine and respiratory care. Teleflex has annual revenues of approximately $1.8 billion, with approximately 12,000 employees operating and supporting healthcare providers in 150 countries.

Telerx is a known leader in customer experience and outcomes, managing inbound call center services and customer service outsourcing. Founded in 1980, Telerx has been successfully building connections and driving outcomes for our clients longer than many of our competitors have been in business.

Tyco International PLC is a security systems company incorporated in the Republic of Ireland, with operational headquarters in Princeton, N.J. (Tyco International US Inc.). Tyco International is composed of two major business segments: Security Solutions and Fire Protection. On January 25, 2016, **Johnson Controls** announced that it will merge with Tyco, in which all businesses of Tyco and Johnson Controls will be combined under Tyco International PLC to be renamed as Johnson Controls International PLC.

As one of New Jersey's largest not-for-profit health systems, **Virtua** provides comprehensive healthcare services to achieve its mission to help people be well, get well and stay well. Virtua provides services through Virtua Medical Group with 302 physicians and other clinicians, and at its urgent care centers, hospitals, ambulatory surgery centers, health and wellness centers, fitness centers, home health services, long-term care and rehabilitation centers, and paramedic program.

A leader in maternal and child health services, Virtua delivers nearly 8,000 babies a year. It provides health services to 1,500 businesses, and participates in Virtua Physician Partners, a clinically integrated network of 1,400 physicians and other clinicians. Virtua is affiliated with Penn Medicine for cancer and neuroscience and the Children's Hospital of Philadelphia (CHOP) for pediatrics. It employs over 9,000 and has been honored as the #1 Best Place to Work in the Delaware Valley every year since 2007. It is the recipient of a 4-star rating from the Centers for Medicare and Medicaid Services (CMS) for quality of care, and its hospitals earned straight A's in patient safety from The Leapfrog Group and the 2016 Patient Safety Award from Healthgrades. *U.S. News and World Report* ranked Virtua's Mount Holly and Voorhees hospitals as High Performing Hospitals and Voorhees as a Best Regional Hospital. Virtua is also the recipient of the Consumer Choice Award from the National Research Corporation. For more information, visit www.virtua. org or www.virtuabroadcastnetwork.org.

About the Authors

Scott Rosen is Founder and President of the Rosen Group, managing the company since 1995. The company has grown over the last twenty years into a leading consulting and staffing firm, providing direct hire and contract placement of Human Resource professionals at all experience levels, specializing in recruiting, compensation, benefits, HRIS, payroll, labor relations, training and development and employee relations. The company's network of talent consists of thousands of highly-qualified, prescreened individuals ready to hit the ground running.

Scott's responsibilities include management, sales, marketing, recruiting, finance, and operations. Additionally, Scott has founded the following brands to support the HR community:

HR Department of the Year Awards (www.hrawards.org)
Human Resources Executive Alliance (HREA) (www.hrexecutivealliance.com)
Talent Acquisition Leadership Alliance

Prior to starting the Rosen Group, Scott spent twenty years in corporate America. The first half of that time was in operations management with Prudential and Cigna, and the second half was spent in HR management as a generalist with Reliance Insurance Company, Travelers Mortgage, and GE Capital. Scott earned his B.S. in Business from Rider University and currently resides in Cherry Hill, N.J. with his wife Risa and their twin children, Lee and Cassidy. In his spare time

Scott enjoys traveling, reading, playing guitar, watching movies, and attending concerts and sporting events.

The Rosen Group
9 Collage Lane
Cherry Hill, N.J. 08003
(856) 470-1399
scott.rosen@rosengroup.com
www.rosengroup.com

***

David Pinette is Senior Vice President with the global outplacement provider Challenger, Gray & Christmas, Inc. Founded in the early 1960s, the firm's primary goal is to assist displaced workers in making the transition to reemployment. It has a proven record of success, conducting fully individualized programs and one-on one consulting for each individual who participates in the process. The firm's clients find new jobs in a median time of 3.2 months, compared to the five months cited by *The Wall Street Journal* as the average length of a job search.

David's twenty years of expertise includes partnering with business leaders and their teams to identify areas of opportunity necessary to achieve performance targets linked to business strategy. His work with Challenger clients has been highly effective in assessing their needs and providing them with tailored solutions to achieve business objectives.

With Scott Rosen, David is a founding member of the Human Resources Executive Alliance, an invitation-only community providing human resources executives in the greater Philadelphia area with a high quality networking and educational experience.

David established the Challenger Executive HR Group of Philadelphia to help support senior level HR professionals in transition, providing them with structure and support in landing their next opportunity.

David is also a partner in the Delaware Valley HR Department of the Year Awards, a prestigious program founded in 1998 that recognizes

HR professionals who have managed change and positive growth. (www.hrawards.org)

He earned a B.A. degree from Bryant University, where he studied marketing and business management.

Challenger, Gray & Christmas, Inc.
1650 Market Street, Suite 3600
Philadelphia, Pa. 19103
Direct (215) 689-0654
Cell (860) 306-3116
davidpinette@challengergray.com
www.linkedin.com/in/davidpinette

***

John V. Touey is a Principal of Salveson Stetson Group Inc. and member of the management committee of the firm, a multi-specialty retained executive search firm based in suburban Philadelphia. Specializing in enhancing leadership capacity, Salveson Stetson Group places senior executives at a wide variety of organizations, ranging from high-growth ventures, to Fortune 500 companies, to non-profit entities. The firm is a member of IIC Partners, one of the top ten retained executive search groups in the world, with 52 offices in 34 countries.

John has more than twenty years of experience in providing executive search, human resources, and management consulting services to a broad range of organizations and industries. At SSG, John manages the firm's financial officer practice and has successfully placed senior level financial executives with several Fortune 500 companies, both in the Philadelphia region and beyond. Additionally, his functional search expertise extends into senior sales and marketing, operations, human resources, technology, and general management roles.

John is a frequent contributor to several business publications and currently serves as a guest columnist regarding career issues for CFO.com. He has also authored articles for TLNT.com and *Brazen Careerist.*

In addition, his work has been cited in *The Wall Street Journal, Barron's, Fortune Magazine, Bloomberg News,* and MSNBC.

Previously, John spent seven years with Right Management Consultants. As Vice President in Right's Philadelphia Regional Practice, he was a major contributor in the development of new human resource and management consulting services for the company. He has worked with a broad range of Philadelphia's leading companies in this capacity.

John holds a B.A. in English from Temple University. He currently serves on the Boards of the Economy League of Greater Philadelphia and the Welcoming Center for New Pennsylvanians. He is a Past President for the Society for Human Resource Management's Philadelphia Chapter and most recently served as the Chair of the Chapter's Senior Human Resources Forum. He is also a past Board Member of the Philadelphia Human Resources Planning Society, the Entrepreneurs Forum of Greater Philadelphia, the Human Capital Working Group of Select Greater Philadelphia, and DPT Business School.

Salveson Stetson Group, Inc.
150 N. Radnor Chester Road, Suite F100
Radnor, PA 19087
Office: (610) 341-9026
Cell: (215) 915-2573
Fax: (610) 341-9025
E-mail: touey@ssgsearch.com
www.ssgsearch.com